Beyond Illusions
Brad Barton

il-lu-sion [i-loo-z*hu*n] – noun

1. An erroneous concept or belief.
2. An erroneous perception of reality.
3. Something that deceives by producing a false or misleading impression of reality.
4. *Psychology.* A perception that represents what is perceived in a way different from the way it is in reality.*

* *Random House & American Heritage Dictionaries*

Beyond Illusions: The Magic of Positive Perception

Published by
Executive Books
206 West Allen Street
Mechanicsburg, PA 17055

ISBN: 978-1-933715-66-7

Credits

Author photo: Derek Smith
Cover Design: Eric Barkle / m2 results / www.m2results.com
Text Design: Eric Barkle
Creative Editor: Tom Cantrell / Tom@TomCantrell.com / 801-355-2005
Edited by: Linda Larsen

Brad Barton Presentations Inc.
2447 Woodland Drive ● Ogden, UT 84403
801-392-4088
BradBartonSpeaks.com
Brad@BradBartonSpeaks.com

Printed in the United States of America

Dedicated to
My Angel Mother

Contents

Acknowledgements

This book has been percolating inside me since God put into my heart the desire to speak. I am eternally grateful to Alydia, my wife, my life, for her belief in me over our wonderful 17-year marriage. I thank my children Jacob, Aubrey, Garrett, Mariena and Sienna May for doing without a lot of Daddy time so this project could be born. "Go Barton Team!"

Although this has been an arduous task, Zane Grey was right, "The difficulty, the ordeal, is to start." Thanks Tiffany Berg for investing so many hours getting me *started*. Thank you Linda Larsen for your many long hours of toil and valuable insight; Rich Hopkins, Julie Meyers and Ruth Jack for excellent last minute proofreading and the team at m2results for your creativity and passion in getting this book *finished*.

Special thanks for their contributions to my wonderful friend, Clifton Taulbert; my hero brother, William and his amazing wife Amber; my delightful sister-in-law Heidi, and my patient and loving Grandmother Sessions - wherever you are.

I acknowledge my fellow speakers and authors, good friends and mentors, Tim Border, Doug Nielson, Kirk Weisler, Jim Ackerman, Jason Hewlett and Chad Hymas – *and the hundreds of you who pre-purchased this book* – for holding my feet to the fire. Thanks also to Brad Montgomery for inviting me to contribute to *Humor Us,* a book that nudged me forward.

Finally, I thank my long time friend, coach, and creative editor, Tom Cantrell for helping me get beyond yet another of my illusions. Words cannot describe my gratitude, so I say simply this: Tom, this book would not be without you.

Foreword

By Tom Cantrell, Creative Editor

Isn't it interesting that a magician would write a book telling you how *not* to be deceived?

It is a very easy thing to be deceived. We all are susceptible. It is important that we understand this. Einstein said, "Understanding the nature of a problem is halfway to its solution."

This book is, therefore, more about understanding problems than about discovering solutions. You will arrive at your own solutions; that's relatively easy. Someone once asked the great Harry Houdini how he got the rabbit out of the hat. He responded, "There is no trick to getting the rabbit out of the hat. *The real trick is getting him in there in the first place.*"

Understanding how our problems are created and perpetuated in the first place, therefore, is the real trick. When we understand how we are deceived, we then have power to no longer be enslaved by the illusions and misperceptions that create personal, spiritual, social and business crises.

When we accomplish this, we have achieved freedom.

Brad and I have dreamed about this book for years and worked on it for more days and long nights than we care to reveal.

Brad had no idea it would be so much work to get his ideas into a manuscript. I had no idea it would be so much work to help him! We have both stretched and grown through this process. The most amazing, magical thing is that we still speak to each other!

I have watched Brad prepare and deliver hundreds of keynote presentations over the past decade. As his presentation coach and friend, I get to see a side of Brad Barton that no one else sees. Those who have heard him speak have benefited from his insightful and inspiring message. However, what you are about to experience goes to a depth that cannot be conveyed in a one-hour keynote presentation. Ladies, you will immediately connect with the spirit and energy of this book. Fellas, if you can get through this book without shedding a tear, you ain't no kinda' man.

Working closely with Brad as a coach and editor has deeply impacted my life. His fun, magical, yet soul-shifting message helped immensely as I struggled through some extremely difficult times. It was empowering to realize that even in the midst of conflict and crisis, if I can manage my interpretations and perceptions, I can maximize my life.

So give this book a careful read and be prepared to look at life – with all its interesting twists and sometimes terrible turns – in a different and more rewarding way. Hope you have as much fun sharing it with others as we have had sharing it with you.

Now, pour yourself a warm drink, settle yourself by the fire, and enjoy what you discover *Beyond Illusions*.

*The work we do 'in' ourselves
is much more significant
than any work we can ever
do 'on' ourselves.*

*I am not discounting the
importance of looking our
best. Neither am I promoting
plastic surgery; after all,
jogging is cheaper and less
risky than liposuction.*

A Weighty Matter

The Art of Guided Perception

"I am an old man and have known a great many troubles, but most of them never happened." ~ Mark Twain

Have you ever created disaster out of nothing but perception? Ever created a *reality* that wasn't *real* even though your *facts* were just as *true* as your interpretation of them – then tried to prove that your disastrous interpretation was true? Confused? Read on ...

My young friend, Heidi, went to a department store to buy a specific type of knit uniform pants required for her new job. She tried on the poorly tailored, tight-fitting, polyester pants, stood in front of the three piece mirror and, to her horror, realized the awful pants made her look fat. In the changing room, she grimly considered her options. Heidi really needed her job, and the pants were a sad requirement; so, she reluctantly took the pants to the cashier. It was mid-December and the store was bustling with Christmas shoppers. In front of the line was an elderly woman asking about a tailored jacket for her granddaughter.

Must be a size 3! Heidi thought, as she watched the sales clerk hold it up admiringly.

Next, two teenagers faced a dilemma about which outfit would look best at their upcoming party and dance recital. Heidi tried to smile at them. *They look absolutely anorexic*, she thought, as she looked down at the polyester pants she was about to purchase. *You'd think they'd make some effort to pick a uniform that looked good on everyone.*

The lengthy wait became more difficult as she observed each thin attractive customer carrying equally beautiful clothes – not ugly ones like the stupid knit pants Heidi was forced to buy. There were three cash registers, but only one clerk; she looked exhausted, but slim and attractive in a blue, belted shirt-dress, which accentuated her waist and made her look authoritative and businesslike.

She's probably the department manager, or at least on her way up the ladder, Heidi thought.

She found herself analyzing every man, woman and child in the store during that twenty minute trek to the check out. They all appeared to possess possibilities Heidi lacked. They seemed more educated, more talented, more attractive, more self-confident and slimmer than Heidi. Finally, there was only one person before her turn to be helped. Heidi's torment was almost over when it got even worse.

A handsome young man, about her own age, opened another register as the first clerk said, "I'm sorry. It will just be a couple of minutes while Jim gets his register going." And she locked her drawer and walked away.

Two more minutes? As if that wasn't enough, now she would be served by a handsome young man with dark penetrating eyes and a smile that could sell anything on the floor. Heidi laid the pants over her arm and started fumbling through her purse for her checkbook so the transaction wouldn't take any longer than necessary. *I think I'm going to be sick.*

"Did you find what you were looking for?" came the clerk's friendly, tenor voice.

Suddenly, Heidi again saw herself in the "fat" pants standing in front of that three-way mirror. *I'm fat. I'm fat. I'm fat!* was all she could think.

The clerk leaned toward her, apologetically, "Ma'am, I am so sorry about your weight."

Shocked, Heidi threw the pants into the startled clerk's face, burst into tears and ran from the store. Halfway home, still in tears, she suddenly realized what the sales clerk meant. This well meaning young man was not criticizing her weight; he was sincerely apologizing for her twenty-minute ***wait!***

Have you ever done what Heidi did? Created a disaster out of nothing but misguided perception? Have you ever taken offense at a co-worker's comment and worked it up in your mind to the level of an in-office Hiroshima? Did you end up feeling embarrassed? Worse, you may have never found out that the offending party was actually innocent and well-intended.

Often, people let such incidents smolder until they fade into the background noise of *why they never liked that person in the first place.* Have you ever negatively interpreted a comment or a look from your spouse, then shot back an emotionally charged reaction that created the very conflict your misguided perception anticipated?

Many of the painful experiences and negative feelings we patiently and nobly endure, turn out to be products of our own making. Our perceptions and interpretations powerfully influence our responses and reactions. All too often, they create the very thing – the very reality – we fear out of (*drum roll please*) absolutely nothing.

You see what amazing wizards we are? We have the power to create our own reality – beautiful or ugly, abundant or sparse – out of nothing more than perception. The question is, if our perceptions and interpretations can create disaster – or the illusion of disaster – can the same power magically create a new positive reality of beauty, opportunity, or even great humor out of the same circumstance? If you possess the ability to create your own reality, then yes, you can create fortune out of misfortune, opportunity out of failure, possibility out of emptiness, and self-fulfillment out of frustration. How? By looking at situations differently. By developing the tendency to look past the conspicuous facts and seeing instead the inconspicuous possibilities.

Bonaro Overstreet said, "No emotional crisis is wholly the product of outward circumstances. These may precipitate it. But what turns an objective situation into a subjectively critical one is the interpretation the individual puts upon it – the meaning it has in his emotional economy; the way it affects his self-image."

You can magically change your life by changing how you perceive events and how you see yourself. This is what I call *The Art of Guided Perception.*

Anaïs Nin said, "People don't live life as it is, they live life as they are" – as they perceive life through the filter of their perceptions, which are based on their attitudes, assumptions, even their expectations. A perception isn't just a thought, it is a special kind of thought. Perceptions are the meanings, the interpretations, placed on our experiences – the things we see, hear, taste, touch, think and feel. Perceptions – the way we interpret facts – control our circumstances and, ultimately, our reality.

James Allen opined that people "… are anxious to improve their circumstances, but are unwilling to improve themselves; they therefore remain bound."

That is pretty heady stuff. So, what binds us? *Our current perception of reality.* Lucky for us, perceptions can change. Once they change, reality does too. Remember, change can be positive or negative, constructive or destructive. It can all start with one small event.

As a boy, I spent countless hours with my big brother, John, irrigating hundreds of acres of feed corn for our family's large dairy farm.

Like every other farm and ranch in the valley, we were allotted by the Co-op a strict portion (shares) of irrigation water on an even stricter timetable. If we missed our time slot, we missed out on the water. One miss could doom an entire field of corn critical to our dairy operation. Neither church nor sleep nor foul weather kept us from meeting that water and coaxing it down the cultivated rows of dark green field corn.

My favorite part was the beginning. The water would come roaring down the ditch like a flash flood.

After we got it turned into its proper channels, and made sure the water was headed down the rows of corn, there were some rare moments of leisure time.

As boys are wont to do, I often entertained myself by playing in the water. I built large mud dams, sometimes two or three feet high, which held back sometimes a hundred gallons or more of irrigation water.

It was an exciting challenge. I had to constantly shore up the dam, keeping the dirt packed tightly to withstand the pressure of the water. This required a vigilant watch. If even the tiniest trickle of water found its way through the thick walls of the earthen dam, the barrier would be compromised and in seconds the dam would collapse and all my hard work would be destroyed in a rush of dark, angry water.

It was fun. It was also powerfully educational. Water always seeks its lowest level and there is constant pressure for it to do so. The same could be said of our self-perception. If we allow even a tiny trickle of negative self-talk to find its way through, it can cut an ever widening swath through even the most solid sense of self-worth, until all we are left with is a muddy hole.

Perceptions are fluid and powerful. Like hydraulic force, they too can destroy – or create. The beauty of this is, like irrigation water, perceptions can be managed by our will to choose.

This is not always easy and it requires a vigilant watch. If left alone, our self-perception tends to follow the path of least resistance and seek its lowest level. However, when we choose to actively guide our perceptions, regularly shoring up our foundation with affirmative self-talk, we guide our present circumstances – or at least our interpretation of our circumstances – and thus change our reality.

In fact, the most important personal change we can make is not to change our work, our financial habits or even our appearance. Actually, the most important change we can make is our perception of who we are, the value we bring to the world and our perception of our own attractiveness.

Dr. Maxwell Maltz pioneered the science of Psycho Cybernetics, the study of how our perceptions of self govern, to a great extent, the results we enjoy from life. Interestingly, he was not a psychologist or psychiatrist. He was a board certified plastic surgeon. During his many years of practice, he discovered an amazing phenomenon. When he surgically improved patients' outer appearance, even subtly, there was often a subsequent and disproportionate improvement in their perception of themselves. This improvement in the way his patients saw themselves created dramatic effects in their lives.

I once experienced this phenomenon first hand.

In college, I dated a lovely young woman named Alydia. Her parents lacked the resources necessary to initiate corrective procedures for her slightly misaligned front teeth. I thought she was beautiful but because of this slight imperfection, she went through junior high, high school, and on to college with a skewed perception of her considerable attractiveness. And so this lovely lady settled for dating me.

Near the end of her sophomore year, Alydia and my best buddy, Lance, were talking. He asked her why she always covered her mouth when she laughed. She tried to side-step his question. He pressed the issue. She then reluctantly admitted her self-conscious feelings about her teeth. At this point, Lance got bold. "If this little thing is creating such a big challenge for you – if it is distorting the way you see yourself – then fix it," he said. "If that means straightening your teeth, then so be it; but get yourself beyond this and start owning the fact that you are beautiful." It was a difficult conversation for both of them, but it set Alydia to thinking.

That summer she found the means to have herself fitted with braces. Almost immediately, her self-image was enhanced. She saw herself as more beautiful and desirable. She finally began to project in abundance the attractiveness she had always possessed. As a result, she became even more attractive – to rival suitors – *even with her braces on.* This because she accepted how beautiful she *really* was (even though I knew it all along!).

What an inconvenience for me! My competition became at once numerous and intimidating. I'll admit to doing the best sales job of my life and, in the end, managed to win her over. It was a close shave. Her name is now Alydia Barton. She has given me three beautiful daughters, two handsome sons and many blissful years of happiness and joy. Her self-image is now a solid one. She reminds me often how fortunate I am that she chose me. I usually just pinch myself and smile in agreement.

Alydia's change in self-image may have caused me some pursuit problems, but that change helped her realize one of the reasons I am so attracted to her. Dr. Maltz called this perception of self, "self-image." As his patients' self-image became enhanced, so too did their social posture. When they saw themselves as more attractive, they tended to project a better feeling about who they were and literally became more attractive. Their confidence, and often even their competence, improved and their lives began to change – like magic. Their lives didn't change because their appearance changed but because their self-perception changed.

Interestingly, not all of Dr. Maltz's patients experienced this transformation. Sometimes even those whose appearance was improved significantly saw and experienced little change. This is because the work we do *in* ourselves is much more significant than any work we can ever do *on* ourselves.

I am not discounting the importance of looking our best. Neither am I promoting plastic surgery. After all, jogging is cheaper and less risky than liposuction. Doesn't it make more sense to work on ourselves from the inside, where change can last, than it does to work on the outside, where change is fleeting at best?

Is it possible that, like Dorothy in Baum's classic *The Wizard of Oz*, we too have been wearing those incredible magic slippers all along? Perhaps we have the power within us now to get beyond our illusions, see ourselves as attractive and come home to that place we have longed to be – pleased with who we really are. Remember the lyric from the 1974 hit by the band America, "Oz never did give nothing to the Tin Man, that he didn't, didn't already have." Tin Man already had a heart, Scarecrow already had brains, Lion already had courage – and Alydia was already beautiful.

If we are anxious to improve our circumstances – if we are anxious to improve ourselves – we must be willing to improve our perception of ourselves. I invite you to take it one step further. If we want to improve our relationships with co-workers and to be closer to our family and loved ones, we must be willing to enhance our perceptions of them as well.

Let's amp it up even more. If we desire to be good and effective leaders, we must also find ways to help others improve their perceptions of themselves and of each other. That is true leadership. That is the power of guided perception.

What did you do when you first heard the clerk's comment about Heidi's *wait*? Were you offended for Heidi's sake? Did you quickly become set in your anger, like most do? Or did you, within seconds, realize that Heidi must have misinterpreted the clerk's meaning because it was just too hard – too unbelievable that the clerk would have said something like that – and, because you tend to give people the benefit of the doubt, your mind quickly scanned for another possibility – a more acceptable interpretation? That is the art of guided perception.

Heidi thought it was real that the young man thought she was unattractive. She acted accordingly. To her great chagrin, it wasn't true. Realizing her mistake, she was embarrassed. Then she was embarrassed about being embarrassed. That made the story even better.

After giving herself time to get over her embarrassment, she began to see reality for what it was. Heidi then could apply the art of guided perception, altering her interpretation of the circumstances, and creating a new reality much more gratifying than the old one.

After all, a misguided reality is never *real* in the first place. Her enhanced perception also eventually guided her to the fact that her situation was, after all, pretty darn funny!

All of us need time to "get over it" when we've been victims of our own misconceptions. Don't try to force an immediate positive perception of a painful experience. Just develop the habit of gently challenging your perceptions when things look bad. Then relax and give yourself time – as much time as you need – to discover the positive reality of the situation. Be like the fellow who sat up all night wondering where the sun went when it set. He waited and waited and waited. Finally, it *dawned* on him.

Monitoring and examining current interpretations, and cultivating and practicing our ability to guide our own perceptions, imbue us with the power to create our own reality; which in turn powerfully, positively and permanently impacts our quality of life, literally changing our lives and the lives of those around us – like magic!

This is the Art of Guided Perception.

"Things may happen around you and things may happen to you but the only things that really count are things that happen in you"
~L. C. Robinson

*Treat them as the magnificent
individuals they really are,
then watch the change occur.
You too will experience the
magic of the Man of La Mancha.*

The Magical Man of La Mancha

I think; therefore, *you* are.

"Where there is great love, there are always miracles." ~ Willa Cather

Can we create our own reality? Can we affect "what is" simply by altering our perception? Can we do it without being considered delusional?

Have you read the classic, *Don Quixote de La Mancha* by Don Miguel Cervantes? Perhaps you've seen the movie. The Hollywood rendition of *Man of La Mancha,* starring Peter O'Toole as Don Quixote and Sophia Loren as the Lady Dulcinea, is incredible. If you haven't seen it yet, put it on your "must see" list. Watch it with your family or a special someone. Or pop some popcorn and settle down and watch it alone. It may well alter how you view "reality."

Don Quixote (a tall, lean, eccentric, retired landowner) perceived himself as a noble knight riding forth on a mighty steed (a broken-down cart horse) to fight evil enchanters and giants (windmills) in defense of truth and justice. His grasp of principle was tenacious. His grip on reality seemed, however, tentative. Quixote saw the world not as it was, but as he perceived it. For this, he was considered insane.

His weakness was his delusion of grandeur.

His greatness was his delusion of *others'* grandeur.

Don Quixote saw greatness in everyone, no matter who they were. Innkeepers were perceived lords of their castles; common folk were noble squires and warriors. Even Quixote's mortal enemies – including a band of cutthroats and thieves – were perceived as excellent worthy opponents on a battlefield of honor.

He regarded a scullery maid, who was also the village prostitute, as a high-born lady of virtue and beauty. He insisted to all within earshot that she was as he perceived her, a lady of magnificence and worth.

This man of La Mancha was a lone voice. He was one rare supportive voice among hundreds of derisive voices – people passing her on the street who knew *what* she was but did not know *who* she was. She felt the distain of polite society – the abhorrence, even vicious hatred, from the "respectable" women in the community. She knew that they were right. Quixote must, therefore, be wrong.

At first she passionately resisted his high opinion of her; angrily insisting that she was nothing and nobody.

"I was born on a dung heap and I will die on a dung heap," she crudely protested.

But Quixote remained steadfast and unwavering in the face of her resistance and ultimately she gave in to his perception of who she really was. She became as he saw her – the Lady Dulcinea.

Was Quixote's high opinion of this common woman delusion or perception? He saw people not as *they* believed they were, but as *he* believed they were. In a day when people questioned not just their worth, but even their very existence, the French philosopher and mathematician, René Descartes, argued in favor of the reality of mankind by saying, "I think, therefore I am." Don Quixote upped the ante. When people doubted their worth, he said in effect, "I think, therefore *you* are – just as magnificent as I say you are."

Because of his unyielding insistence, they ultimately gave in to his perception of their greatness – *his* delusion of *their* grandeur. This unlikely hero had the gift of true inspirational leadership. Common folk actually became great because of Quixote's "delusions" about them. His delusions were no longer delusions; they were perceptions – and his perceptions became reality.

This crazy visionary rejected "reality" as the worst possible illusion. In its stead, he imagined a new existence and made it come true through the sheer force of his will – or better yet, the magical power of his positive perception.

Quixote wasn't just some poor wandering vagrant. He was a wealthy and successful landowner who, as he grew older, realized more and more the sorry state of the world he lived in. He called the oppressive negative reality that others saw, "a stone prison crushing the human spirit" and he set forth with banner, buckler, shield, and lance on an old broken-down cart horse, to alter that reality.

Though he saw none, he believed in justice and mercy. Though he despaired at the wickedness and cruelty of his fellows, he believed fervently in the nobility of humankind. When others mocked him and called him mad, he replied, "*The greatest madness is to see life as it is, not as it should be.*"

Quixote's amazing if seemingly insane ability to see others, not as they saw themselves, but as he saw them, created a new reality; a reality more promising, more productive and more practical than the old one. His insistent perception of others' greatness and inherent goodness *changed* circumstances by transforming people who *create* circumstances.

As he did, so too can we. Perhaps the highest indication of true leadership is to inspire greatness in those around you *by perceiving them as magnificent and wonderful, despite how they may appear or behave in the moment.* Touting our own greatness may be egotistical, but regarding others positively inspires greatness in them and can literally change them – consequently changing "reality" – just like magic.

So, back to the original question: Can we create our own reality? Can we alter "what is" simply by altering our perception? Yes, we can – and we do. When we enhance living breathing human beings by enhancing our perception of them, and consequently their perception of themselves, we enhance the circumstances they affect. We go *beyond illusion* and enhance reality. We make our world what we choose it to be through the exercise of our *power of positive perception.*

Some believe you cannot change others; you can only change yourself. Is this true? Ask Don Quixote. Ask Dulcinea. Ask my dear friend, Pulitzer Prize nominated author, Clifton Taulbert ...

Marked for Good

as told by Clifton Taulbert

*I*t was on the Mississippi Delta in the 1950's; the place and time of separate and very not equal restrooms, restaurants and schools. I was a small boy. I didn't understand discrimination, but I felt it. My world was defined and hemmed in by racism, cotton plantations, plain board floors and oil lanterns – and mud and dust and worn out overalls ...

... and a wonderful old man standing in the doorway to our poor home. He had a book held reverently in his hands from which he read ideas that I had never before heard or dreamed – an old man whose name I sadly do not remember.

He lived in a place called the Colored Colony and was known simply as "the book reader." It was a term of distinction. Reading was an uncommon skill in a world where a man's worth was usually determined not by his ability to work through rows of words on white pages of a thick book but by his ability to work through white rows of thick cotton.

He lived in a small "shot-gun house" – one of those two-room homes scattered by the thousands across the southern landscape like cracked wheat in a hen-yard. He collected and read books; all kinds of books from all sorts of authors. His big iron bed with the scrollwork and bars that looked like a cage without walls was surrounded by books. In fact, the space was so small, not much else could garner room. Yet, it was in this small and cramped environment that he unselfishly sought to change our view of ourselves – and prove to us somehow that our cages also had no walls. We only had to open our minds to the wonderful world drawn on the pages of his books.

The old man was not just a reader; he was a visionary. He saw a wonderful future — for me.

Every Saturday, every summer, all summer, he would dress up in his best and only worn wool suit. Stuffing a dozen of his books in a tattered leather bag, he would make his way to Glen Allan, our small Mississippi Delta Community. The long and dusty walk under the hot southern sun left him with a blazing thirst. Upon reaching my great-grandfather's house, he would ask for water in his halting, stuttering voice.

Poppa would go out back and get him a dipper filled with water from the pump hydrant and chipped ice from the ice cellar. After a long drink, and a moment to catch his breath, the old man would peel off his hot suit coat and thoughtfully select from one of his precious books just the right one for this day. He would sit and talk with us, and any adult who would listen to his stuttering but erudite thoughts and proposals of perception and possibility. Shakespeare hath never been stuttered so well.

This wonderful nameless old man, this self appointed open air librarian, gave us a picture of ourselves that didn't just hint at, but pointed with the finger of poets, prophets and philosophers, to life beyond the fields of the Delta – and to our own hidden but very real potential.

Upon completing his reading, he would get up to leave. But before leaving, always he would look us in the eyes and touch each child and tell us in his precious stutter, in that voice that had become the voice of Melville and Dickens and Carroll, that we were indeed "marked for good."

Today, I travel throughout the world enjoying a life beyond the wildest imaginations of the children of the Delta who grew up in the legally segregated South. But it is not beyond *my* imagination, because this wonderful old man planted these dreams deep in my soul. He taught me possibilities instead of poverty and, when I am reminded of the many people who poured hope and dreams into my life at a time when our world was defined by racism and cotton plantations, I am particularly reminded of one unnamed old African whose life defied the times and more particularly the prejudices and limitations of those days.

I am the author of twelve books; one nominated for the Pulitzer Prize, and have lectured on the "Power of Community" to members of the United States Supreme Court. I have served as a guest professor at Harvard University's Principals Center and I have taught leadership to organizations around the globe.

I am grateful beyond expression to this wonderful nameless old African man – the reader of books; the teller of stories; the lantern bearer who stood by the open door of my young world and whose words of affirmation and promise pulled me through and locked the past behind me. His stuttering voice became part of my life – a constant subconscious inner voice that molded my destiny and directed me to a life of rich abundance – all because he took the time to read to me, fill my thoughts with beauty and promise and, more than anything else, blessed me every week of every summer of my young life by touching me and telling me that I was "marked for good."

Clifton Taulbert was indeed "marked for good" and his life was forever changed for the better. Who in your life has done for you what Don Quixote did for those around him – and what the book reader did for my friend Clifton? Who has said on your worst day that you are great and good and, though you resisted, you changed – sometimes in that very moment?

Look around you; not just now, but every day. Look at those no one else is looking at; and look at them in ways no one else sees them. Believe what you see is real. "To believe your own thought," said the introspective Ralph Waldo Emerson, "to believe that what is true for you in your private heart is true for all men, that is genius."

An American writer once interviewed British Prime Minister William Gladstone. When ask what he thought of Gladstone, he replied, "He is the most interesting person I've ever met." Years later, this same American spent time with Prime Minister Benjamin Disraeli. When asked what he thought of Disraeli the man replied, "He made me feel like *I* was the most interesting person *he* had ever met."

Benjamin Disraeli exemplified the spirit of Quixote when he wrote, "The greatest good you can do for another is not just to share your riches, but to reveal to him his own."

Have you ever done this for someone else when they did not believe in themselves – and neither did anyone else? Are you willing to be that lone voice of approbation? Then grab your Quixotic lance and shield, and wrest someone from his or her dung heap. Challenge their reality. Tell them the truth about themselves, even if they protest. Treat them as the magnificent individuals they really are. Then watch it happen. Whether slowly or quickly, it surely will happen – the magic of the Man of La Mancha.

"Each one sees what he carries in his heart" ∼ *Johann Wolfgang von Goethe*

*I didn't intentionally choose
my new perception.
Life handed it to me as a gift.
When it happened,
I accepted it and my life
was made richer for it.*

That Was Snot a Bad Deal

There is nothing good or bad, but *perception* makes it so.

*"It is not how much we do, but how much love put to the doing.
And it is not how much we give, but how much love we put into the
giving."* ~ Mother Theresa

*I*t was one of those days, a crash and burn day. Nothing had gone right and I came home unhappy, frustrated, crabby and annoyed. I realized that if I remained upstairs with my family, I was going to infect them all with my negativity. Attitudes are, after all, contagious. So, I made the noble choice to remove myself to my downstairs office. (Okay, what really happened was my wife banished me, "Get downstairs, Brad! We are getting sick of your attitude!")

I grumbled my way to my office, feeling misunderstood and unappreciated. After a few minutes of feeling utterly sorry for my-self, and getting very little accomplished, I heard the pitter patter of little feet on the stairs.

I looked up to see my five-year-old, Jacob, negotiating his way down the steep staircase. "Jacob, get back upstairs," I growled, "Dad is not in the mood to talk to you right now."

Jacob didn't hesitate. He trotted right up to me and said emphatically, "Dad, I gotta talk to you."

That's when I noticed that Jacob had a cold – a really messy cold. It was literally all over his face. Allow me to describe this in better detail so you will understand what I was dealing with. He had a big thick trailer hangin' out of one nostril, well past his lips. As he sputtered excitedly, trying to tell me whatever it was he just had to tell me, that thick tendril stretched between his lips like greenish-yellow taffy. The other nostril exuded a bubble of green ooze which moved rapidly in and out with every excited breath as he tried to tell me what he had to say.

I sat there staring at him in utter disgust thinking, *whose kid is this?*

Did I mention I was not in a good mood?

"Daaa-a-d" he insisted, "It's really, really 'portant. I gotta talk to ya!"

I put down my pen, swiveled my chair toward him, leaned over and curtly said, "WHAT?"

My messy little five-year-old stretched up on his tiptoes, grabbed me by the ears in a death grip and pulled my face within an inch of his own. He quickly licked my right eye and then my left eye, and exclaimed "I love you Dad!" Then he took off, running.

I sat there, stunned, with his slimy green snot all over my face.

Jacob raced back up the stairs, yelling, "Momma! I did just what you told me!" (What? She was in on this? I was already furious at Jacob. Now there are two people in trouble!) "I licked Dad right in the eyes and said, 'I love you, Dad!'"

"You did *what?*" exclaimed my wife, in disbelief. "I told you to go downstairs and *look* your dad in the eyes and tell him you love him."

I stumbled to the bathroom, shaking my head. As I washed the virus-ridden mucous from my eyes, I began to laugh – really laugh – deep-down, soul-cleansing laughter. I laughed 'til my gut ached. It felt wonderful. Extra oxygen flowed, endorphins were released, my energy surged and my perceptions changed – *like magic!*

I dried my face and went upstairs in a completely changed mood. I went looking for my little Jacob. He had retreated into hiding when he realized his blunder. I picked him up and hugged him. He wrapped all four limbs around me like five-year-olds do, and hugged me back. The feeling of love and gratitude that swept through me was pure magic. I stood there in awe, realizing what a wonderful gift I had received from what any rational person would say was a pretty bad thing.

I thought to myself that no matter how grown up this little boy gets, maybe with a son of his own someday, from this night on he will always be my very own little Jacob-man who, on a very bad day, "licked me in the eyes" and told me he loved me – and magically changed my perception and my reality. That evening is now a cherished memory, mucous and all. That is the magic power of positive perception.

About 48 hours later, I came down with a really nasty cold. I had three miserable days at home in bed to consider how licky, uh, I mean lucky, I truly am.

Is reality set and real or is it fleeting and subjective? Is the way I perceive the world right now really the way the world is, or is this just my current perception?

Often what is perceived as real is not in agreement with the true facts in the environment. Spin yourself around quickly ten times and the room starts to spin – but is it really spinning? Stare at a revolving disk with a spiral design on it and you will perceive movement that isn't real. Sit in a car at a stoplight and, if the car beside you starts to roll backward, you get the physical sensation that your car is moving forward and you instinctively press harder on the brake.

In this respect, "reality" is not "real." Your car is not moving regardless of how "real" that movement feels. What if we could intentionally alter our perceptions and our reactions *and our results* – by intentionally deciding what is real – rather than simply accepting the obvious?

Shakespeare wrote, "There is nothing either good or bad, but thinking makes it so." I suggest similarly that there is nothing good or bad, but *perception* makes it so. If I decide that a *bad* situation is actually in some way *good* – then it is. Real magic is our ability to change – to turn a bad deal into a good deal – simply by changing the way we look at it. That is the power of positive perception; and it is powerful magic.

In this messy little interaction with my five-year-old son, I didn't intentionally choose my new perception. Life handed it to me as a gift, and I accepted. I would never have consciously decided to change my perception about getting slobbered on. I certainly never would have thought it a "gift"! However, when it happened, I accepted it and my life was made richer for it. If life has the power to create serendipity (a fortunate desirable discovery), isn't it possible for you and I to perform this same trick on purpose?

Does this story of mine feel familiar to you? Has life ever dumped on you and, at some point, you realized it was a load of diamonds?

*E*arly on in my academic life, I realized I was not like the other kids. I struggled to read, to write, to spell and to understand mathematics. I was subsequently diagnosed with dyslexia, a learning disability. This was real blow to my self-esteem and it lead to a destructive perception of my talents and capabilities. For years I held a poor opinion of my potential.

When I was a collage freshman, my English Lit' professor Dr. Westfall, a man I had come to deeply respect, asked to speak with me, privately. He spoke optimistically about dyslexia and specifically about the gifts he saw in me. That conversation reframed in my mind what dyslexia is all about. It had an enormous impact on the way I viewed my so-called learning disability. I began to experience hope; hope for my present and hope for my future. He also mentioned, as he handed back my first paper, that since I was now in college, I should learn how to spell it. In editing this section, my editor caught a particular spelling error. You're right, I misspelled "college."

Years later, I read the book *The Gift of Dyslexia* and came to more fully appreciate the gift this supposed disability really is. In his insightful book, Ronald D. Davis writes, "Dyslexia is the result of a perceptual talent, an asset which in some situations becomes a liability." He reveals that this multi-dimensional visually fixated perception style creates the vulnerability for confusing symbolic information processing. Davis added, "It can also make people imaginative, inventive, able to think on their feet and react quickly. They are often good athletes, conversationalists and storytellers."

Imagine my relief to learn that Hans Christian Andersen, Bruce Jenner, Alexander Graham Bell, George Burns, Cher, Winston Churchill, Leonardo da Vinci, Walt Disney, Albert Einstein, General George Patton, William Lear, Charles Schwab, Woodrow Wilson and Jay Leno are all dyslexic – just like me! Where once I saw liability, I now see opportunity because I began to elevate my thinking, look with a different set of expectations and create a better paradigm.

Stephen Covey says it this way, "It isn't what happens to us that affects our behavior. It is our interpretation of what happens to us. And when we can learn to get a better paradigm – get to a different level of thinking – then we are on the road to significant improvement." He calls this the essence of self-determination.

I call it the Power of Positive Perception.

My wife calls it Magic.

"*The problem is not that there are problems. The problem is expecting otherwise and thinking that having problems is a problem.*" ~Theodore Rubin

Believe in magic.
Not rabbits coming out of
hats magic, but real magic -
magic that comes out of
challenging our
interpretations of reality
to choose a perspective
that creates more options
than might first appear.

The Poisonberry Perspective

Seeing Without Vision

Pearls lie not on the seashore. If you want one, you must dive for it.
~ Chinese Proverb

*R*ecently, I was having a polite but intense "discussion" with my normally very sweet wife. I, of course, was right. She, of course, was wrong.

My five-year-old, Marina, who had been watching the interchange from a safe distance, interrupted, "Daddy, why don't you just say you are sorry and then be happy like you usually are?"

How could she say such a thing? No way could it be that simple – but it was. What we were fighting about simply wasn't worth fighting about. Art Linkletter was right. Kids do say the darnedest things – and sometimes they are darned right. Sometimes they speak with the wisdom of Solomon (or at least one of his kids). While it is true that kids do sometimes say amazing and insightful things, I will go out on a limb here and say that isn't the norm.

Often we sit dumfounded and wonder what planet they came from, whose language they have been learning, and from whom.

When my Aubrey was four years old, I learned a valuable lesson about human perception and how what we observe and accept unchallenged often limits our opportunities – and we don't even realize how much.

Kids sometimes come up with the dangedest observations you ever heard because they are observing from their limited perspective – the Poisonberry Perspective.

*I*t was a picture-perfect late summer evening in beautiful northern Utah. Aubrey and I were in our garden picking berries for my wife's famous cobbler. My baby girl was "helping," as only a four-year-old can. Curiously, however, she wasn't sampling the berries as four-year-olds do. As we filled her little blue tin bucket with big juicy dark berries, she looked up and said, "Daddy, we can't eat these berries, huh!"

Somewhat taken back, I said, "What do you mean, 'Bree-girl? We are going to eat them. Momma is gonna make yummy cobbler with them tonight and we'll have 'em for dessert."

"But Daddy," my precocious but perplexed little girl said with grave concern in her four-year-old eyes, "we can't eat them. They are poison."

I didn't understand at first what she meant, then it dawned on me; "Oh, no, Honey, these are not *poison* berries, they are *boysen*berries."

"Oh," she said, matter-of-factly, and we resumed picking berries (she still wasn't sampling them).

A few minutes later, our task complete, we headed for the house. As we neared the back porch she hesitated, "Daddy, why come *I* can't have these boysenberries?"

Again confused, but knowing better than to assume anything, I asked, "Why do you say you can't have them?"

"'Cause I'm a girl," she said.

Now fully confused, but hangin' on for the ride, I ventured the logical question, "Why does being a girl keep you from having dessert with the rest of us?"

Looking at me as if I had nothing but dust in my brain pan, she said, "'Cause, Daddy, you said these are *boy*-senberries."

That's when I turned her, her little blue bucket of berries, and her questions over to her mother.

Young children believe what they see and hear, don't they? They tend to interpret information quite literally. They question but rarely challenge the facts. Perhaps that's because a child's limited experience limits their perspective and they don't look very far beyond the facts of the moment. This limited view – this looking at life in the immediate is what I call, *The Poisonberry Perspective.*

Isn't it the same with adults? Like children, don't we frequently react to our observations (actually our *perceptions* of our observations) as though they are real, without looking very far past the obvious "facts?" We often don't even realize we aren't thinking about what we are thinking about. This doesn't serve us very well.

There is an enormous difference between thinking something - and thinking about thinking about it. It is one of the great gifts of being human. We are not only aware, but we are aware that we are aware. We can, therefore, challenge our own perceptions.

When my Aubrey was looking with limited perspective, she thought the berries were poisonous and thus limited herself from sampling a very flavorful piece of life. However, when she started asking questions (when she started challenging her perceptions), she finally began to understand on a higher level and was able to enjoy more fully the bounty that life offers.

So, what are we looking at with limited perspective? Do we ever suffer from the Poisonberry Perspective? Does that limit our reality – our opportunity to enjoy a bigger slice of life?

At least my little girl had the wisdom to question her perceptions; and I had the wisdom – to turn her over to her mother!

It's silly for us to think that children could think the silly things they think because we adults often do the same silly thing. We allow our immediate sensory *experience* to limit our *perspective*. Things that seem good are good – and things that seem bad are bad. I mean, it just seems so obvious.

Our interpretations may be from a sensible perspective – after all, we did see what we saw. We heard what we heard. We certainly felt what we felt. But those interpretations may be coming from a limited perspective – the Poisonberry Perspective. Even though they are rational, even reasonable, assumptions – they may be inaccurate.

The *Screwtape Letters*, by beloved author C.S. Lewis, is a story about the working conditions in Hell. Screwtape is an experienced tempter who advises his nephew, Wormwood, through a series of diabolical letters, how to gently manipulate someone into the infernal regions. It is a fascinating treatise on the art of deception from the perspective of the Master Deceiver and his lesser imps.

One particular letter of instruction speaks to the issue of reality and the importance of *limiting a patient's perspective* in stealing away the freedom to choose.

> My dear Wormwood … By the very act of arguing, you awake the patient's reason … you have been strengthening in your patient the habit of attending to universal issues and withdrawing his attention from the stream of immediate sense experiences. Your business is to fix his attention on the stream. Teach him to call it "real life" and don't let him ask what he means by "real." … don't let him consider realities he can't touch and see.

So, again, what are you looking at with limited perspective – the Poisonberry Perspective? Stop reading for a moment and consider this important question: How has your attention to *the stream of immediate sense experience* limited your perspective and kept you from seeing what is real?

Adults have a much larger store of information and experience to draw from; and yet, like children, we often rely on limited interpretations. This leads us to believe that things that seem good *are* good; and things that seem bad *are* bad. Our interpretations may be from a sensible perspective, but a limited one – the Poisonberry Perspective.

Shakespeare wrote, "There is nothing either good or bad, but thinking makes it so." I prefer to say it more simply, "There is nothing *bad,* but thinking makes it so." Bold statement? Not really.

Recently I enjoyed lunch with a long time friend, Vance Anderson. This is no ordinary man. He once finished third place in the Boston Marathon, has been ranked in the top four in his class in U.S. Archery Competition, is an amateur magician and an accomplished musician, served as clergy for his church congregation, earned a masters degree and built a successful private counseling practice. He is a popular inspirational speaker, the father of two daughters, and has been married for 38 happy years.

Vance is also a paraplegic – has been since his youth.

It is very easy to think that his experience (the weightlifting accident that caused his paralysis) was a disaster, especially the day it happened. I would have thought so. Vance did. But he hadn't yet lived long enough to know the outcome. Now he has. Years later, sitting there in his wheelchair, Vance set me straight.

"Brad," he said thoughtfully, "before my accident, I was headed down the wrong road. I shudder to think what my life would be like if I hadn't broken my back."

Was the accident that paralyzed Vance a disaster? Yes, it was a disaster – from the Poisonberry Perspective; but not from Vance's perspective. And he ought to know.

As a keynote speaker who frequently applies the metaphor of magic, I have learned that in the mind of my audience perception is reality. A skilled magician can manipulate even a sophisticated skeptical adult audience into believing all kinds of things that simply are not true. All the magician has to do is limit the audience's perspective and divert them from challenging that perception. If I can do this to my audience then it's all over but the Shazaam. With stage magic, this is fun. In life, it is limiting and sometimes dangerous.

In the movie, *Merlin*, the young wizard is courting his lady love. He reaches into the night sky and takes the full moon into his hand. The sky darkens and moonlight glows through his clasped fingers. Then he puts the moon back in the sky. As the sky lightens, his lady sighs in wonder and says softly, "That's magic."

Merlin quietly responds, "No, that's just a trick. Magic is real."

Magic *is* real. In fact, magic is more than real. Magic is the power to change reality by creating new facts. I am not talking about changing events. I am talking about changing perceptions about events, which create new realities with new opportunities.

Much of what we perceive as negative is illusion. The circumstances, the events themselves, may be real, but our interpretation of them as negative, could that be an illusion?

*I*t was April 1970. The Apollo 13 mission was in trouble. A crisis jeopardized the lives of the entire crew. The obvious fact was that this was a bad situation. What wasn't so obvious was that this apparently "bad" situation was a call to greatness that was answered by everyone involved.

As the spacecraft approached the Moon, at a distance of 199,990 miles from Earth, the number two oxygen tank in the service module exploded, setting at risk the mission and the lives of those on board.

John Swigert, Command Module Pilot, immediately contacted Mission Control, calmly under-stating, "Okay, Houston, we've had a problem here."

Mission control responds, "This is Houston. Say again, please."

Commander James A. Lovell affirms, "Houston, we've had a problem."

The oxygen tanks on board the craft needed to be stirred at certain intervals to prevent the oxygen slush from stratifying. Damaged Teflon-insulated electrical wires powering the stirrer motor sparked and the volatile mush exploded, destroying critical equipment and power supplies. The landing at the Fra Mauro Highlands was abandoned and the mission aborted.

The complexity of the problem and the immensity of the danger could not be overestimated. The crew and flight control had to exercise tremendous creativity under extreme conditions to jury-rig the craft for the crew's safe return. This required considerable ingenuity under incredible pressure while the world watched the developing drama on television.

In the Movie, *Apollo 13,* we knew there would be a successful ending because, well, it was a movie. Tom Hanks would surely bring 'em home. But this was real life. There were no guarantees of success. In fact, it is reported that when the President of the United States demanded to know the odds, a ranking NASA official gave the astronauts a dismal one-in-five chance of survival.

That thought was nowhere more poignantly felt than on the spacecraft itself and in the homes of families and close friends of the astronauts.

In the movie that recounted the adventure, when the NASA director lamented, "This could be the greatest disaster NASA has ever experienced," NASA Flight Director, Gene Kranz, refused to see the obvious. He would not even consider the possibility of a disaster.

He responded, reflecting Winston Churchill's comments during the apparently disastrous but ultimately victorious Battle of Britain, "With all due respect sir, I believe this is gonna be our finest hour."

In his book, *Failure is not an Option*, Kranz recounts the bold and inventive solutions to problems that ultimately brought the crew safely home. What could have been NASA's worst disaster was tackled with the same constructive perspective and subsequent presence of mind as did Winston Churchill, in WWII. Facing the Battle of Britain, he announced to the House of Commons, "This will be our finest hour." Gordon B. Hinckley, author of the book *Way to Be* explains:

"If ever there was a man who demonstrated this, it was the Prime Minister of England, during World War II, Winston Churchill. The year 1940 was a desperate time when bombs were falling on London. The German war machine had overrun much of Europe and was moving into Russia. Most of Europe was in the dread grasp of tyranny, and England was to be next. In that dangerous hour, when the hearts of men were failing, and when fear gripped everyone, Churchill spoke, saying,

> 'Do not let us speak of darker days; let us speak rather of sterner days. These are not dark days; these are great days – the greatest days our country has ever lived and we must all thank God that we have been allowed, each of us according to our stations, to play a part in making these days memorable in the history of our race.'

Like Churchill, Gene Kranz didn't just "think positive." He recognized that circumstances which appear disastrous and desperate – even hopeless – could be more constructively perceived as opportunities for greatness. (In fact, you can hardly find an opportunity for greatness that does not at first appear to be a disaster!) Like Churchill, Kranz knew that circumstances do not govern end results; it is our perception of circumstances that governs end results.

With the power of positive perspective, the challenge was met. The NASA ground crew, astronauts, and support personnel looked beyond the obvious and achieved a successful resolution – a victory which proved the apparent disaster was, in fact, "their finest hour."

We must have adversity and challenge if we are to realize our potential. Who would Nelson Mandela be without apartheid? Who would Abraham Lincoln or Clara Barton be without the

Civil War? Who would Winston Churchill be without the threat of the Third Reich?

Who would we be without the challenges that have revealed our strengths? Who would any exemplary soul be without the apparent disaster that brought that soul to greatness?

So, are disasters really disasters? It depends on your perception.

Believe in magic; not rabbits that come out of hats magic, but *real* magic – magic that comes out of looking beyond the obvious facts and challenging our interpretations of reality.

What if we accepted the idea that our immediate interpretations of our circumstances – "our stream of immediate sense experience" as Screwtape calls it – is probably not accurate? What if we rose above the *Poisonberry Perspective* and chose a higher perspective – one that recognizes more options than might at first appear?

What if we exercised the creativity of the Apollo 13 team, under extreme conditions, and kept our minds open to the idea that our interpretations of difficult situations – even apparent disasters – are probably inaccurate and therefore limiting?

We would realize the wonderful truth that any difficult situation, even an apparent disaster, could be our finest hour. It all depends on our perspective.

> *"Discovery consists of seeing what everybody has seen and thinking what nobody has thought."* ~ Albert Szent-Györgyi

*To assume without
examination that a difficult
experience is bad
denies the wisdom of a loving God
and the power of the human spirit.*

That's Good. That's Bad.
That's *Funny!*

Just because it stinks, is it rotten?

> *"Mind is the master power that molds and makes; and man is mind, and ever more he takes the tool of thought, and shaping what he wills, brings forth a thousand joys, a thousand ills. He thinks in secret and it comes to pass. Environment is but his looking-glass."*
> ~ James Allen

In the 1950's, business philosopher Earl Nightingale, pioneer of the personal development industry, father of portable PMA (Positive Mental Attitude on records and tapes), said that we can turn a bad situation into a good situation simply by reinterpreting it. He suggested that when something bad happens, even something really bad, we should speak the magic words, "That's good!" and then get to work figuring out what's good about it.

Try it – right now. Think of a situation that you think is bad. (An employee from Fright Night files a grievance; your 16-year-old son comes home from a date and asks if the car is insured; the transmission drops out of your RV the day after the warranty expires; your doctor asks, "Do you have a will?") Have you brought to mind a bad situation? Okay, now say out loud, "That's good."

What's the matter? Maybe you're thinking, "That isn't realistic. It isn't good. It's a bad deal. It's rotten. It stinks! It is a very bad deal."

Of course it looks bad. It certainly isn't much fun. But, even if something hurts, even if it really kicks you in the gut, could it possibly also be good, even very good? I didn't say you had to like it. I merely asked if it is possible that something that looks really bad could be perceived as really good – even before you know how it possibly can be good.

Remember the common phrase of the 1990's: "It's all good." Could they (we) have been right? Just because it stinks is it rotten? Even if it is rotten is it bad?

Have you ever lost a job – a really great job? You were devastated. Then you began a career that is much more rewarding – something you never would have had the guts to go after if you hadn't been forced to by a "bad deal." You now enjoy a career that you wouldn't have *found* if you hadn't *lost* the job!

Ever had a bad employee? It's miserable isn't it? Did dealing with it motivate you to create better hiring processes, better training, and more legally defensible systems that ultimately enhanced your production and profit?

Ever been dumped? Was your heart so completely broken that you wondered if you could even make it through another day? It was awful, wasn't it! Then, later, you looked back and realized that things turned out so well you are amazed at how blessed you are – perhaps you are now in a relationship that is deeper and much more fulfilling than that old one ever would have been – and you think to yourself [whew], I am *so* glad I got rid of her (*or him!*).

Sometimes life plays what seem to be some pretty nasty tricks which, by a wonderful turn of fate, turn out to be unexpected magic. We gain serendipitous gifts of good fortune directly from apparent bad fortune. If life can do this by chance, can you and I create this same kind of magic on purpose?

Wayne Dyer said emphatically, "Our intention creates our reality." We can orchestrate good results directly from difficult, even painful circumstances when we recognize that bad situations don't *provide* opportunities; bad situations *are* opportunities. Every enlightened business leader knows this. Bad situations – even really bad situations – are opportunities to gain understanding, improve relationships, invent new services, and enhance products and profits.

In 1982, Tylenol capsules were poisoned – loaded with cyanide by a still unknown social terrorist. Several people died. In 1993, meat products in some Jack in the Box restaurants were tainted with harmful bacteria as a result of a supplier's negligence. Hundreds were sickened. Three children died.

Can you imagine how the leaders of these companies felt? Not only were they reasonably concerned for the future of their companies, they were deeply saddened because of the human tragedy. How these two companies handled their respective tragedies is a model of corporate responsibility and higher level thinking.

Company leaders realized their disaster was also their opportunity. Even though the safety of their products had been seriously compromised and the resulting tragedy could have spelled the demise of their corporations, the responsible and sensitive way these corporate executives handled the crises enhanced their reputations and raised industry standards for product safety and quality control that today protect hundreds of millions of consumers.

As a direct result of Johnson and Johnson's quick and open response to the public panic caused by the poisoning of their Tylenol Extra Strength Capsules, there is probably not a bottle or box of medicine on the shelves of North American food and drug stores today that does not have safety features invented or inspired by the makers of this still popular and trusted pain medication.

In a 1999 Business Digest article, "How 'Jack' Turned Crisis Into Opportunity," Jon Entine wrote:

> Jack in the Box not only survived this horrific crisis; they have since experienced an unprecedented revival. What makes this story unique, however, is not the company's crisis-management tactics, but how the genuinely horrified company executives transformed this devastating crisis into an opportunity to remake its entire corporate culture and reawaken a near-comatose brand. Jack in the Box is now considered an industry leader in safety and health procedures, not because of great spin control, but as a result of changes throughout the company."

The Hazard Assessment Critical Control Point system (HACCP) for food safety "from the farm to the fork" created by Jack in the Box in the aftermath of their tragedy is now recognized by the USDA as a model of safe food handling and processing for the restaurant industry. The Washington DC-based consumer group, Center for Science in the Public Interest, also recognized Jack in the Box for its leadership role in food safety.

These two companies could have been destroyed by these corporate and personal tragedies; instead they became recognized industry leaders in product safety. They enhanced the standards of the industry itself because they recognized that their respective tragedies were also opportunities. In responding positively to those opportunities, they earned greater respect and customer loyalty than they ever would have, had the disaster not occurred.

The crises that threatened their very existence and created such great sorrow and loss for the affected families became an opportunity that made these companies leaders in their fields. It inspired them to create and promote safe products and systems that protect hundreds of millions of lives every year. This is especially significant considering the threats that face America today.

It has been said that hidden within every tragic death there exists some elements of good. When that good is discovered and benefited from, honor is brought to that person. What discoveries have you already experienced as a result of a painful loss? What growth and gain, though wrought through sorrow and pain, is yet to be uncovered?

When even very painful and tragic circumstances present themselves, we can see them as opportunities to enhance our lives and perhaps the lives of others in ways that would not have been possible had those events not occurred. If, whenever something really "bad" happens, we transform it into something really good, wouldn't that be really great?

In the year 12 B.C., Horace wrote, "Adversity has the effect of eliciting talents, which in prosperous circumstances would have lain dormant." A financial setback can lay the foundation for financial security by motivating greater financial responsibility. A serious illness can cause one to re-evaluate priorities and gain increased satisfaction and deeper meaning in life. It can also lead to more healthy choices and consequently a longer, higher quality life. An intense conflict with a loved one can ultimately enhance understanding, increase loyalty, and take a couple to a greater level of intimacy and understanding.

It is axiomatic that tough experiences, handled well, enhance our lives. In fact, we are generally closed to better options when we are satisfied with our current situation. Typically, we will not search for a higher path as long as the path we are on is comfortable and easy to negotiate.

Where is that higher path? It's not *out there*, it is *in here*. It is inside our hearts and minds. Viktor Frankl said, "When we are no longer able to change a situation we are challenged to change ourselves." And how can we change ourselves? By changing our interpretations – our perceptions. This is not just about being *positive* this is about being *causative*. A causative agent is someone who creates or *causes* positive change through the deliberate use of the power of positive perception. This process is more – much more – than just being positive.

Now don't get me wrong, I like positive people (I consider myself a member of their tribe). Genuinely optimistic people help us feel good about ourselves and hopeful about our possibilities. Besides, they are more fun to be around. The greatest among us need positive people in their lives. Consider the greeting on Wayne Dyer's telephone answering system:

> *This is Wayne Dyer that you've reached and I want to feel good. If your message is intended to do anything other than that, then you've reached the wrong number and I suggest you call Dr. Phil.*

So *positive* is great, but *causative* is greater. Perhaps the best way for us to start feeling good, even in "bad" situations, lies in our willingness to look at words like *tough, miserable, painful, devastating* and understand that they are not the opposites of *good*.

> If we do not adopt the right outlook, it is possible that anything and everything could cause us frustration… By bringing about a change in our outlook towards things and events, all phenomena can become friends or sources of happiness, instead of becoming enemies or sources of frustration.
> ~ The Dali Lama's Book of Wisdom, 1999

In the small Idaho town, near the cattle ranch where I spent my formative years, there was an old 4X4 pickup truck with a two word bumper sticker that read, "Events Occur." Okay, I edited this a bit. The actual words are "Sh___ (Stuff) Happens" (okay, more editing). Have you seen this particular bumper sticker? Of course you have. Is there an element of truth in this rather pessimistic in-your-face slogan? Of course there is. However, some adopt this as a philosophy of life, spend their days proving themselves right, then wonder why their life is so full of (uh) stuff.

Many times things happen to us that are obviously positive. Like when some wonderful apparently undeserved gift from the cosmos lands in our lap. (Ain't it great?!) We have also suffered painful set-backs. *Stuff* happens that causes trouble, discomfort, even great agony; kicks us square in the solar plexus and knocks the wind out of us.

But is this <u>bad</u>? It feels bad, it looks bad, it might even smell bad, but is it by definition *bad*?

I am not saying that tragedy never occurs; nor am I suggesting that when it does, we should ignore it and pretend that it is not unpleasant and difficult – sometimes even horribly painful. We cannot press blissfully onward pretending nothing ever goes amiss – because it does.

But is it bad?

In the final analysis nothing is "bad" unless we give up and let it be "bad" – and let it stay "bad."

*I*n a concentration camp in Nazi Germany, Psychiatrist Viktor Frankl chose to challenge his obvious perceptions. Instead of focusing on the horror of everyday events and experiences, he chose to look deeper. He faced tragedy head on, found new meaning in human existence and later formulated a method of treating patients that stemmed directly from his astonishing epiphanies discovered in some of the most horrifying circumstances imaginable. In his most famous book, *Man's Search for Meaning*, Frankl writes:

> ... everything can be taken from [us] but one thing: the last of human freedoms – to choose one's attitude in any given set of circumstances, to choose one's own way... to decide how you want to perceive circumstances, rather than just adopt the interpretations that others promote or even what your own experience proposes, but instead make a conscious decision to make a better choice regardless of how unreasonable that choice might seem.

> In the concentration camps there were always choices. Always another opportunity to make…a decision which determined whether you would or would not submit to those powers which threatened to rob you of your very self, your inner freedom; which determined whether or not you would become the plaything of circumstance…

When we are no longer able to change a situation – we are challenged to change ourselves.

When life deals us a blow and we accept responsibility for finding good in it, we shift from being a victim of circumstance, to being a causative agent. This place of free will is a difficult but richly rewarding place to live. We advance from being simply positive to being causative.

Blessedly, we are not forced to endure the same traumas Frankl did, but opportunities for growth and freedom disguised as "bad situations" face us every day. There are always choices to make – always opportunities for us to make decisions which determine whether we will *become the plaything of circumstance* or to enhance our perceptions, see the possibilities and live in freedom.

Frankl surmised that, "Between stimulus and response, there is a space. In that space lies our freedom and power to choose our response. In our response lies our growth and freedom."

What if our response to any tough situation is, "That's good?" That is what Nightingale suggested and it is essentially how Frankl responded to horrifying circumstances. Then Frankl wrote a book about it. *Man's Search for Meaning,* has sold over nine million copies so far, has been translated into 24 languages and voted one of America's ten most influential books by the Library of Congress. Frankl's book changes the world as it shifts the common perceptions about adversity in the hearts and minds of the millions who read it.

Can you think of a good practical reason to believe that good comes from every difficulty or tragedy? How about this: *tough stuff is going to happen regardless of how we decide to regard it.* We can curl up in a corner and try to avoid it. We can resist it. We can endure it. We can bury it. We can regret it and hate life because of it. We can even choose to go about life as if it hadn't happened. Or we can change our perspective, search for the good in whatever happens and accept the truth told by Paul the Apostle, "… these things shall all work to your good …"

Early in this chapter, we surmised that sometimes pretty nasty stuff, by a wonderful turn of fate, turns out to be serendipitous gifts of good fortune. So what then is "serendipity?" The dictionary calls it "luck or the gift of finding valuable or agreeable things not sought for." M. Scott Peck in *The Road Less Traveled*, adjusts the definition slightly but powerfully:

> … let us redefine serendipity not as a gift itself but as a *learned capacity* to recognize and utilize the gifts of grace which are given to us from beyond the realm of our conscious will (emphasis added).

With this *learned capacity*, and through the gifts of grace, we can discover for ourselves value in even the most difficult of life's challenges. In his timeless classic, *The Greatest Salesman In The World*, Og Mandino wrote:

> … I perceived, at last, that all my problems, discouragements, and heartaches, are, in truth, great opportunities in disguise. I will no longer be fooled by the garments they wear for mine eyes are open. I will look beyond the cloth and I will not be deceived."
> ~ The Scroll Marked IV

We were preparing the third edition of this book for publication when I received a call from my editor. "Brad," Tom said excitedly. "I just gave a couple bucks to a fellow sitting on the sidewalk asking for handouts. Brad, he's got a handwritten sign that reads, 'Anything is a Blessing.' How cool is that?"

Now clearly the man meant any contribution, no matter how small, anything at all, would be a blessing. He obviously didn't mean that being down on your luck – especially being homeless – is a blessing; but is it – or could it be?

This man who had apparently been humbled by life to the point of begging was more right than he realized. Anything *is* a blessing – *anything at all* – illness, accident, injury, bad luck – even homelessness – is a blessing; or can be, depending on how we look at it, respond to it, learn from it and grow from it.

Okay, maybe you don't want to call that really tough situation you are in right now a blessing. I understand. I probably wouldn't either. How about calling it an opportunity? That works for me; after all, what are opportunities if they aren't blessings?

The point is, anything is, in fact, a blessing, depending on your perception and your perspective.

On second thought, maybe I do that man a disservice. Maybe he meant exactly what he said, "Anything is a Blessing;" the fact that he was alive, the fact that he knew that humanity cared enough to help him out. Even with all the suspicion and distrust directed at beggars and strangers, he knew that there were enough people out there who would take care of him.

Maybe he really didn't need their money at all.

Maybe he wasn't homeless.

Maybe he was a messenger.

When my editor was going through a particularly tough time, he wrote, "We think of our universe as perfectly balanced – but it is not. It is tilted, slanted and unbalanced – positively. The positive imbalance of the universe is that no matter how devastating the destruction, or how terrible the tragedy, it is heavily outweighed by the lessons learned, the growth experienced and the wonderful stories told."

You see, we don't just get lessons and growth and strength out of the tough stuff of life. We also get an abundance of wonderful stories; stories of valor, strength, grit, heroism, and humor that warm the heart and encourage the soul; stories that elevate us and help us see beyond our immediate circumstances; stories that help us appreciate the wonder of our possibilities. Through these wonderful stories, stories like that of Viktor Frankl, perspective is enhanced, lives are changed and the world advances.

So how do you feel about Nightingale's advice? When something difficult or painful happens, instead of saying, "That's bad," try saying, "That's tough," "That's painful," or "That's difficult." Isn't that actually more accurate? Isn't it also more practical?

Then follow this up by saying, "That's good," and you will begin to see how accurate and practical that is as well. Don't second-guess this. Don't try and figure out what's good first, and *then* call it "good." To get some real magic going, look at your situation honestly and acknowledge how tough, disappointing, miserable, or painful it really is. That's the obvious part. Then do what isn't so obvious. Say "That's good" – say it out loud – and see how that shifts your energy.

Then watch how that energy shift puts you in a different place – a different level of thought – maybe even a different mood. From that more creative perspective, you will be empowered to discover what is good about it. You also will find that you are not alone in this place of power. The Creator, whose very nature is good, is in that place with you.

Historically, people all over the world have united and changed lives in positive and beautiful ways as they respond to tragic or horrific events. Whether it is an attack on Pearl Harbor or the World Trade Center, or the devastation caused by the natural forces of hurricanes and tornados, or even the emotional pain of a family in crisis, people have the power to transform adversity.

President Bush, referring to the attack on the World Trade Center, called it an "adversity [that] introduces us to ourselves." Billy Graham said it was "a tragedy that could have torn us apart; instead, it has united us."

Some things are tough, painful, difficult, miserable – even horrifying. But we don't know enough yet to know if they are actually bad. We haven't lived long enough to know the ultimate outcome.

To assume without examination that something is bad assumes it shouldn't have happened. This denies the wisdom of a loving God and the power of the human spirit. It denies the *power of positive perception.* No matter what happens – it is good when you cultivate the right attitude and use your causative power of positive perception to energize you and help you see past your present circumstance, into the place of power and promise that lies *beyond illusions.*

I have made some pretty bold claims here. I have concluded that no matter what happens – it is good. I am not the first to say this. Earl Nightingale said it. Billy Graham said it. The Apostle Paul said it.

Is this hard to take? Is this pretty tough doctrine? If you have suffered a tragedy, this may seem too big a pill to swallow. If so, don't go there yet. Try this idea on little things first, inconvenient things, tiresome situations. See how it works. Notice how this approach changes your mindset. As you experience benefits from applying your new insight perhaps you will feel inclined to apply it to the tougher stuff life dishes out. It may not always be easy to look at life this way, but it works. If you are going through a particularly harsh situation, I hope this encourages rather than offends you.

We strive for peace. We work for prosperity, and when life is disrupted by destruction and death, we naturally react with anger and sorrow – even long-lasting depression – especially when we just can't make sense of it. The greater the devastation, the greater the anger and the deeper the sorrow. But, with all due respect to Rabbi Kushner, author of *When Bad Things Happen to Good People,* I suggest that bad things don't happen to good people. Inconvenient things, troubling things, painful things even horrifying things happen, but nothing bad.

How can I say that there is nothing that is bad? Because bad is not a *thing*. It is not a thing and it is not an event – and it is not a condition. *It is a perception.* Good is also a perception. So let us entertain the perspective that "it's all good" as long as we are willing to perceive and proceed accordingly.

Remember, this is not a new idea. Not only did Shakespeare suggest the same thing, he was preceded by a couple of centuries in this philosophy by Chaucer. Consider this archaic, but oh so true, statement from Chaucer's Canterbury Tales:

> Thanne is it wysdom, as it thynketh me,
> To maken vertu of necessitee,
> And take it weel that we may nat eschue,
> And namely that to us alle is due.
> [Then it is wisdom, I think,
> To make good things out of bad.
> And take trouble well, that we may not forgo
> Those good things we have coming to us.]

Psychotherapist, speaker, and close personal friend, Doug Nielsen tells of twin sons raised by an extremely abusive father. One was resourceful, happy and successful, the other, broken, miserable and imprisoned. When asked why they turned out the way they did, each had the identical response. "You would have too, with a father like mine."

Does this mean that disaster, devastation, or divorce is good?

By itself, no. It means that when "bad" happens, we can hope for – even depend on – good things to come out of it, and that we will reap the rewards. Why shouldn't we? We have already paid the price in pain.

What if you can't see right away what good will come from a tough situation? That's okay. Perhaps if you can't call it "good" right away you can call it something else ...

When I was eight years old, my Grandmother Sessions came to live with our family. As a young woman, Mae Alice Maude Quick Sessions had immigrated to the United States from South Africa. She retained her rich South African accent throughout her life. She also retained her wonderful sense of humor.

In her very old age she suffered from chronic headaches. Loud noises, like my eight rambunctious brothers, sisters and me wrestling and fighting, made her headaches worse. She especially hated our music. She called Rock 'n Roll "That damnable boom, boom, boom!"

Grandma had been with us eight years when my sister Julie and her three-year-old son Jason came home to live with us. Jason was spoiled rotten. When he didn't get his way – which was often – he'd throw himself on the floor, limbs flailing, exuding high-pitched screams. These outbursts would send Grandma's headaches clean off the pain chart.

After months of mounting tension, my grandmother finally exploded. She screamed for my mother at the top of her frail lungs, "Maaa-a-a-ry, get in here!"

My Mother rushed in to find Grandma in her favorite yellow chair, beet red with anger. In her elegant South African accent she yelled, "I cannot stand it any longer! This house is too small for the both of us. One of us has got to go; it's me or that boy."

Mother calmly walked to the adjoining bathroom and began to put water in the tub. She then walked back into the room and calmly asked, "Mother, would you like a little bit of water or a lot of water in the tub?"

My confused grandmother stared at her; then countered, "What do you mean? You gave me a bath this morning!"

Mother explained, "Jason is little; and to get rid of him only takes a little water. If we are going to get rid of you, we'll need the whole tub full – your choice."

They stared at each other for a few tense seconds; then they both burst into laughter. They laughed until they thought their sides would split. Grandma's headache disappeared, like magic – at least for the moment.

Comedian Michael Pritchard said, "Laughter is a bit like changing a baby's diaper. It doesn't fix the problem permanently, but it makes everything okay – for a little while."

The facts at the Barton home hadn't changed, but perceptions had. Jason's outbursts still caused Grandmother great pain, but in one good fifteen-minute belly laugh a whole summer of stress and anxiety was swept away.

After that, when things got really tense, Grandmother would simply yell, "Maaa-a-ry, fill the bath all the way. I am ready to go now!"

As a professional speaker, I have the privilege and power to alter perceptions in the minds of audiences around the world. I use the metaphor of magic to challenge old beliefs and perceptions and create new insights; empower corporations and educators; and, best of all, entertain and inspire thousands of individuals.

It's great fun to dazzle a crowd with seemingly impossible feats of magic. But it is even more fun – and fullfilling – to move them *beyond illusions* and empower them to create their own reality through the *magic of positive perception* ...

... and sometimes the powerful, positive shift in perception from "that's bad" to "that's good" requires first shifting from "that's bad" to "that's funny"!

"Everything is funny, as long as it's happening to somebody else."
~ Will Rogers, 1879-1935

There is evil in the world.
There are flat tires and nasty neighbors.
That is a fact.
But facts make up only 10% of reality.
Perception is the other 90%.

The Prize

Where there's 'Will,' there's a Way

Know ye not that they which run in a race, run all; but one receiveth the prize – so run that ye may obtain. ~ I Corinthians 9:24

*H*ave you ever considered the anatomy of a bad day? Sometimes your day gradually builds negative momentum until it turns into "another one of those days." Other times a "bad day" is borne of a single disastrous event that leaves you feeling demoralized and discombobulated. In either case, there comes a time when your day appears to spiral out of control, morale plummets and a helpless, hopeless feeling takes command. You are hydroplaning; you apply the brakes, crank the wheel – and nothing happens. It is this feeling of powerlessness, not the events themselves, that defines a "bad day."

Charles Swindoll said, "... life is 10% what happens to me and 90% how I react to it." I prefer to say it this way, "Life is 10% what happens to me and 90% how I *respond* to it."

When Viktor Frankl wrote of his experience in surviving the holocaust, he said that instead of focusing on the horror of every day events, we have the power to choose our response; and "in our response, lies our growth and freedom."

What happens when I accept greater responsibility for my day? My focus shifts from what happens to me (the 10%) to my vast ability to perceive, interpret, consider and thoughtfully respond (the 90%) and I become more powerful as a result. I then set my own pace, run my own race, and obtain the prize – freedom.

This is no easy trick. Living in the 90% – that place of responsibility – is painful. I generally do not like pain; therefore, living in the 10% seems the easier choice. In his incredible book, *The Road Less Traveled*, M. Scott Peck says, "Billions daily attempt to avoid the pain of responsibility, by escaping from freedom." My Eastern Kentucky friend, Chuck Burton, says it like this, "People run from responsibility faster'n a scalded dog."

When we focus on the 10% (what happens to us) and just sit in it, bemoaning our fate and not move into the 90% (what we can do about it), we give what happens to us much more weight than it deserves. We then remain helpless, hopeless, victims of circumstance. We lose the greatest prize of all – freedom.

Many there are who focus on the 10% and give up their capacity to be agents unto themselves. This is no way to live.

As Paul wrote to the Corinthians, "Know ye not that they which run in a race, run all; but one receiveth the prize – so run that ye may obtain." And how do we run so that we may obtain the prize of freedom? It's not easy. Running in a race is painful. Accepting responsibility is painful. Life can be painful, especially if you have fallen from a tree on a cold winter day, and lie paralyzed in the snow.

*I*t was Christmas Eve, 1988, on the family ranch at the foot of the beautiful Bitterroot Mountain range near Salmon, Idaho. Actually, it was Thanksgiving weekend, but it was Christmas for us. For the first time in years, the entire Barton clan was gathered in one place; so we declared our own special family Christmas celebration. This was quite a crew, nine siblings – some of us with spouses and children.

It was a special day on the ranch as well. It was weaning day. We looked forward to the major events on the ranch, calving, branding, weaning, and the cattle drive up Main Carmen Creek to the summer pastures. These events were a lot of hard work, but they had always been family times. My brothers and I spent that bright clear Saturday morning in the saddle rounding up the cattle and separating the nearly grown calves from their mothers.

The rest of the day wasn't so glamorous. The weather turned and we endured a cold wet snowy afternoon, running 300 angry mother cows one-by-one through the cattle chute. They needed their yearly shots, parasite treatment, de-horning and … well, you just don't wanna' know the details.

We were just finishing up the day's work. I was attempting to cut a damaged ear tag off an especially ornery cow when she threw her head at just the wrong moment and I felt the blade slice clean to the bone of my left index finger.

As I headed for the ranch house for treatment, I sent my little brother, William, and his wrestling buddy, Matt (yes, nicknamed "Wrestling Mat") to harvest the family Christmas tree for our evening festivities. I'd looked forward to going with them, but was now in no shape to make the trip. I watched with envy as Will drove the GMC truck we called Whitey over the snowy hill and out of sight. I then retreated to the house and got busy getting my finger sewn back together by my sister Julie (nothing like good ol' country home medicine – at least she is a nurse). Later, I was lying on the front room sofa trying to deal with my throbbing, bandaged finger when Will's friend Matt, burst through the back door.

"Come quick," he gasped, "Will's hurt!"

Matt's tears had iced on his face from running two miles through frozen Idaho woods. The wild panic in his eyes erased the pain in my hand as my brothers and I grabbed coats and hats and piled out of the house toward the old fence-mending truck, a sun-faded grey '63 Dodge. It had no doors and it had no starter. It was parked on a hill behind the house so it could be coast-started.

We got it rolling. Kevin jumped behind the wheel and threw it into gear. It skidded a few feet while the cold engine turned over, caught and sputtered to life. Semi-frozen gravel spurted from under the old truck's rear tires as Kevin gunned it and tore out of the driveway.

Suddenly, he slammed on the brakes! Our sister Julie was chasing after us waving her arms frantically and yelling, "Get a stretcher – it might be spinal."

A stretcher? On a ranch? In Idaho? Heck, we were just reconstructing my finger with adhesive tape, 4 lb test fishing line and a curve needle saved from a veterinarian's C-section procedure. Where would we get a stretcher? A quick search uncovered a partial sheet of heavy particle board half buried under a pile of wet scrap lumber near the granary. We threw the board into the truck, with some old bed sheets with which to secure William, and headed out.

Will had wanted to find the perfect tree for this special Christmas; and he found it – growing from the top of an ancient Douglas fir beyond the far corner of the ranch in a place we called Christmas Tree Canyon. He had climbed 40 feet up the tree and had just finished cutting off the top, when the cold-brittled limb he was sitting on snapped, pitching him into a slow reverse summersault. Breaking limbs with his body as he fell, he landed headfirst onto the frozen ground with only four inches of snow to cushion his fall.

In his panic, Matt had lost track of where he'd left my brother. We tried to follow their old tracks in the snow but found only a meandering crisscrossed trail created as they had searched for that perfect tree. Our efforts wiped out what trail there was with our own footprints.

It was growing darker. Frozen tree limbs stood starkly against the dimming sky. It was bitter cold and getting colder. Our weakening yellow flashlight beams searched the snow-punctuated shadows, creating their own dark and confusing shapes. We grew frantic.

After a heart pounding seemingly futile search, I stumbled onto Will's still form. He was gasping for breath. His neck was broken. He lacked the strength to call out to us because his intercostal muscles were paralyzed. The only thing keeping him barely breathing was his still functioning diaphragm muscle.

Together we quickly considered our situation and sorted out our options. We secured his head and neck as best we could and carefully hoisted William onto our makeshift stretcher. We strapped him onto the particle board, stabilizing him with the bed sheets and got to work figuring a way out of that steep snowy little canyon. It is a very good thing to have brothers that can be counted on.

Do you remember the 1990's CBS program, "Rescue 911" hosted by William Shatner? This long-running popular docudrama portrayed amazing real-life rescues that captured the hearts and minds of a generation. If you were one of the millions who tuned in, you may have seen the re-enactment of this cold, dark "tragic" night on the Keystone Ranch near Salmon, Idaho. The uniqueness of this episode wasn't only that it was a difficult rescue, but that it was carried out completely by our family with no professional guidance, except for our sister, Julie, a Registered Nurse. There was no "911" system in our little rural community at that time and calling for the local volunteer Search and Rescue team would have taken time. We didn't have time. We had to get Will down the mountain.

Our options looked bleak. There was no way we could negotiate the steep, slick terrain above or to each side. Our only real choice was to haul Will down slope and make our way as best we could up the brushy canyon bottom. It wasn't pretty. We fought our way over tangled deadfall, between tree trunks, and through dense willow branches. Wild raspberry and current bushes tore at our faces as we carefully forged ahead up the less severe grade.

William was cold – very cold. He grew less and less responsive as his core body temperature dropped further. We knew that time was of the essence as our frozen fingers fought to hang onto the corners of that slick damp scrap of lumber we called a stretcher. My big brother John was near collapse from utter exhaustion. Kevin, Rick, Alan and I were not doing much better. There wasn't enough strength left in us to negotiate the slick snow and brush encumbered terrain.

In desperation, Alan suggested that we needed help from a Higher Power. The lot fell on me to lay hands on Will and ask a blessing on him and on the group. We knelt in the snow around Will's semi-conscious form and pleaded for help from the only One who could hear us out there. That's when we realized we weren't alone. Something in each of us shifted, especially in John. Today, we all remember the struggle before the blessing. We don't remember any pain or exhaustion after. Somehow William hung on. We made it out of Christmas Tree Canyon, back to the truck and on to Steele Memorial Hospital in Salmon.

At the hospital, emergency attendants cut off Will's frozen wet clothes and began to raise his body temperature by packing hot blankets next to his hypothermic body. A portable x-ray machine was wheeled into the trauma room. A few minutes later, in the adjoining room, Dr. Boyd Simmons flipped on the light behind the x-ray image. I felt as though I'd received a stout blow to my solar plexus. The x-rays revealed that Will's neck was not only broken, but that his c-4 and c-5 vertebrae were crushed and shoved completely out of alignment.

I felt sick.

Doctor Simmons examined the x-rays carefully. He took a deep breath, turned to my mother and quietly said, "I am so sorry, Mary, your boy's spinal cord is severed."

He paused. He could read in my mother's eyes her unspoken but desperate question. He took another deep breath. Very gently, with all the compassion he could muster, he continued, "He will never feel or move anything – from his neck down – for the rest of his life."

That's a pretty tough 10%.

I belong to a church with a lay ministry. Boyd Simmons was not only our family physician, he was also our minister – our Bishop. Mom knew that he would never say anything like that if he didn't really know that the situation was hopeless.

It sure looked like a pretty bad deal.

I can't describe the sheer torture Will went through for the next many weeks.

It was physical torture. The striker frame with metal tongs pulled his neck into alignment with constant traction. A halo brace with four screws through the skin into his skull, held his head in place. He suffered complete immobility, atrophy, dysreflexia, muscle spasms, excruciating neck pain and massive headaches. It was ten days before Julie was even allowed to shampoo the dried mud, blood, tree bark and dead pine needles from his matted, curly hair.

Worse than the physical pain, though, was the mental torture. The shock. The unfolding realization of what had happened and that there was no going back. He'd awaken from dreams of running or wrestling and re-experience the shock of it all. This modest country boy had to deal with the humiliation of catheters, bedpans and nurses. He watched his perfect All-State athlete body atrophy. He suffered the agony, grieving and fear of a life imprisoned in numb flesh. Despair was his constant tormentor, along with the horrific question, "Why?"

We did what we could to support and cheer him. When he was rotated face down, our older sister, Mary Jo, would climb under Will's striker frame with her baby daughter, Emma, to cheer him, share stories and wipe tears from his eyes and nose.

It wasn't just torture for Will. This trial deeply affected our family, our church and our little community of Salmon, Idaho.

His tragedy was ours ...

... so was his triumph.

After being stabilized in the trauma-care unit in Missoula, Montana for two weeks, Will was transferred to the 6th floor on the south wing at McKay-Dee Hospital in Ogden, Utah – the spinal injury rehabilitation ward. I participated in the tag-team round-the-clock family vigil. (Large families can indeed be a blessing.) I often took the night shift. Many of those first nights, I slept on a portable cot next to him in his hospital room. We didn't want him to be alone when he awakened, which he often did, startled by a strange hospital noise, a persistent itch on his forehead or chin that his paralyzed hands couldn't scratch, or a pleasant dream of winning a cross-country race, or tossing one of his big brothers off the haystack.

One night I was awakened by muffled sobs. I sat up. "What's going on, buddy?"

Tears poured from his eyes. "Think - I'll ever get - married?" he whispered past dry lips. "Think - ever - I'll have a son – maybe?"

A sixteen-year-old kid shouldn't have to be worried about things like that.

I wish I could tell you that I jumped out of my cot that night and stood over him, looked him straight in the eye, and said, "Of course you will, little brother. You're gonna be fine. Everything's gonna work out. You'll see. You got magic!" But I couldn't – because I didn't believe it myself. All I could do was hold my little brother's lifeless hand, wipe the tears running into his ears, and weep with him.

Those weren't fun days for Will – or for any of us. What followed were weeks of misery, desperation and despair. Then, like a fresh wind blowing in from the sea, something shifted. Will died.

*I*t happened like this. One day, a hospital staff member, who was unfamiliar with the physiological challenges that face quadriplegics, blew cheerfully into Will's room and said, "C'mon we're going to sit up today."

Without thinking, he cranked Will's chair and Will – for the first time since his accident – into a straight upright position. Will's blood pressure plummeted, his respiration ceased and he died. Will tells it like this:

It was a particularly bad day. How any day could be worse than all the others, I don't know, but this day was. I had just abruptly ended a phone call with my big brother, John. I knew I had hurt his feelings but I was overwhelmed with self-pity and just didn't want to talk to anyone. I watched this guy come toward me with a big stupid grin on his face saying that he was going to sit me up. I tried to tell him, "No, I can't do that!" But the guy ignored me. As he abruptly inclined the adjustable back support, I felt the blood drain from my head and everything faded to black.

My next recollection was of floating near the ceiling watching it all happen. I saw the panicked aide searching desperately for a pulse and screaming for help. As he began CPR, the room became a blur of activity, but it all seemed so far away – detached and unimportant.

I turned and became aware of a familiar space. It was the place my mother and I had created in my mind through the process of visual imagery in the days immediately following my fall. Many times in the previous weeks when despair had taken over, she and I had retreated to this beautiful garden sanctuary, a time-out place free from the horrors of reality, safe from worry, pain and care. It was a place to run and move and be free.

I entered and walked deep into the garden. The brightly colored flowers, fragrant punch of ripe fruit, and the soothing sound of distant running water drew me onward. Time had stopped and I was at peace. I realized with certainly that if I reached the far boundary just beyond, I would never have to return. I could just keep going past and on into the next realm. The attraction was nearly overwhelming. It would be so easy to cross over and turn my back forever on a bleak reality. My heart leapt. The most wonderful feeling of peace and love passed through me. This was the way out I'd been praying for. I could just quit.

Then the thought struck like an arrow to my heart. I can't quit. That's not who I am. For me, quitting is unacceptable. My mind flashed back to the previous August, a defining experience I'd had on a hot dry afternoon on Carmen Creek road.

I was on a run with my big brother Brad, training for the upcoming high school cross-country season. We had logged a lot of miles that summer between irrigation duties, fence mending and the busy haying season. For weeks, Brad had tailored my training, steeling me for this one special workout. He called it the Power Run. It was ten miles of torture designed for pain and intended for growth. Brad promised me that if I could complete this run at this pace, I was on track to earn All-State cross-country honors. Early on, I knew I was in trouble. The pace was lethal, and by the halfway point my legs grew weary and my heart began to doubt. Brad's reassurances kept me on course for four more grueling miles as I struggled to keep my focus and stay positive.

With less than a mile to go, victory within sight, I fell apart. My breathing became labored, my eyes filled with tears of emotion and pain. My will broke. I had never realized what they meant when athletes referred to "hitting the wall" I thought that's what was happening. Brad knew better. He knew there was more in me. I fell off the pace and then collapsed into a gasping heap at the side of the road.

Brad called after me, first in encouragement and then with some sting. "I never thought I'd see my little brother quit," he yelled as he ran on toward the finish.

I lay there in real pain, struggling for breath. Then something within me awakened. I saw it all clearly. The pain, the trial, the discipline were all part of a greater purpose, a refining process meant for growth and self-mastery. This was my defining moment. Would I lay there and quit, back down and give in, or would I get up and face head-on the very struggle my big brother had designed especially for me to forge me into the runner I was meant to become? It was only a few seconds, but that moment of self-reflection defined me and prepared me to meet the challenge of a lifetime. Me quit? No way! I got up and sprinted through the pain. The look on Brad's face as I pulled even with him at the finish was priceless.

I did earn All-State honors at the Idaho State Cross-Country Championships that fall – just like my big brother said I would.

Now I was faced with a similar choice. I could walk away from the challenge, leave my family, forgo the stifling pain and set this tremendous burden down. All I had to do was give in and quit. Me quit? No way! I would loose the prize. I would forfeit the growth, the wisdom, and the contribution I could still make in the world. Besides, I owed my big brother John a return phone call.

The choice was mine. I chose to live.

The hospital lights, noise and confusion returned as Will returned to consciousness – as physically disabled as ever, but now enabled – empowered with new vision – new perception. Will calls this his "near-*life* experience." He says this was as near being truly alive as he has ever been. While technically unconscious – he was fully conscious of his purpose – this experience permanently altered his perspective.

One day, soon after, I was spending time with him in his hospital room, when Will strained his eyes to meet mine and quietly said, "Brad, I chose to climb that tree ..." there was a long pause, then he added earnestly, "... and I now choose this as my life – and I intend to make the most of it."

After weeks of despair, enduring his role as a helpless hopeless victim of horrible circumstance, Will shifted his focus away from the 10% and chose to live in the 90s.

Years later, after the funeral of a young family friend, several of my siblings lingered at the wake. Together they mused on the tragedy and fought to understand the meaning of it; how painful and difficult life can be and how unfair it all sometimes seems.

Seated in the corner, listening carefully to the discussion, my wise quadriplegic brother at last quietly spoke. "Life is supposed to be hard. That's why we are here – to experience and grow and learn *and appreciate how wonderful it all is.*"

There is evil in the world. There are flat tires and nasty neighbors. There is trauma and tragedy, like falling out of a tree on a cold snowy day and landing on your head. That's a fact. But facts make up only 10% of reality. Perception – and the way we apply our perception – is the other 90%. It is in the 90s, this place of power, we gain the prize – freedom!

William had some difficult days after that; he still does. We all do. But never again did William Barton beg his mother to end his life as he had so many times during the first weeks following his fall. He was finally at peace, even though neither he nor his family had given up on the idea that he could and would walk again.

The citizens of our little town of Salmon, Idaho asked their friends and family to join in a day of community fasting and prayer, and it didn't stop at the borders of Lemhi County. It became international and interdenominational. Catholics, Episcopalians, Mormons, Lutherans, Jehovah's Witnesses, Jews, Buddhists, Baptists – they all prayed for William.

The day immediately following the ecumenical fast, Will's little toe moved – and so did the hearts of his family – his entire family – a few thousand of us – world wide. Let me clarify; Will's toe didn't just move; William moved his own toe on purpose (well, to be fair and honest, he didn't do it by himself; he did it with a whole lot of help from a very powerful God). Will was a tiny bit less paralyzed than he had been the day before, but oh, what a difference that tiny bit was. What followed was a rapid reawakening of entire muscle groups on the left side of his body. The Neurosurgeon said it was a miracle and told the family not to get our hopes up.

Don't get our hopes up? *That's how we got a miracle!* Almost immediately, Will's right side started waking up as well. This was not a "rise up and walk" miracle. This was a try and fail and try again, struggle to move, spill all over your shirt as you try to feed yourself kind of miracle; the kind that very slowly makes an athlete, a star – a real man – out of a 16-year-old grappler (wrestler).

Long months went by – purposeful months dedicated to resurrection and restoration. Will now wrestled as he had never wrestled on the mat. Nothing worked right. His therapists strapped eating utensils to his hands and constantly adjusted them as he exercised his slowly rejuvenating body. He would break a sweat just sitting up; but, sit up he did, over and over and over again.

Months of therapy ensued, involving specialized gloves, spoons, combs, tooth-brushes, and a wheelchair with knobs on the rims, so he could gain traction with the heels of his numb hands.

While I was running laps in the WSU Dee Events Center across the street, with my college track coach pressing me for higher performance, Will was doing laps around the sixth floor of McKay-Dee Hospital in his wheelchair with his therapist. I was working past my limits. Will was working beyond his limitations. I was getting faster. He was going farther. I dreamed of being an NCAA All-American. Will dreamed of being able to walk. There is no question who the real athlete is.

Eight months later doctors removed Will's halo brace and released him. He wheeled slowly out of the hospital and into the real world. He suffered neck pain, severe headaches and nagging general discomfort. His dream was to walk again; but the insurance money was exhausted – no chance for rehab' – now what?

Mom and Dad learned of a bodybuilder in Provo, Utah who worked with quads on the cheap. They scraped together a few dollars and drove Will to Provo. As Will struggled through the door in his wheelchair, he literally ran into a huge foul-mouthed bruiser – a man who obviously took no prisoners. With this man, you either succeeded or - or - - - hm-m-m-m - - - come to think of it, there was no "or" – you just succeeded. That was it – and Will did. He wheeled in and – seven months later – he left without the wheelchair.

Almost 18 months from the day Will fell from the tree and became "hopelessly paralyzed" he walked across the stage and graduated with his high school class.

Let's back up. That sounded too easy. It wasn't. Not by a country mile it wasn't. Will was still a quadriplegic. He did walk across that stage but not quite like the other graduates. He lurched, limped and struggled across the stage as our hometown audience jumped to their feet and clapped and cheered and wept. They stood and applauded the fact that Will, too, was standing.

Fast-forward a few years. Will decided to go to college. Mom decided to make it happen. It did. He earned a Mathematics and Information Technology degree from Idaho State University. He then began a career working on the IT team at a large hospital in Idaho.

Then Will decided to answer that important question he'd asked me that terrible night so many years ago as he lay weeping in his hospital room ("Do you think I'll ever get married and have kids?"). It was no easy task for him to find a wife. It had to be someone with some wit. You have to have a sense of humor to date a Quadriplegic. Amber has a great sense of humor. Will and Amber became Mr. and Mrs. William E. Barton.

Ten months after they married, the second half of that question was answered. Amber gave birth to their first son. Fifteen months later, she gave birth to their second son. Eleven months later, she gave birth to their third son. Fifteen months after that, she gave Will their fourth son. As of this writing, Amber is minutes away from delivering son number five. Amber is beginning to lose her sense of humor.

Life is far from easy for them. They struggle when the 10% of life happens to them. Will's hands don't work very well. He tires easily. He has fallen and broken his nose many times over the years, and recently endured painful nasal surgery so he could breathe more comfortably. He stumbles a bit and his knees are wearing out from walking the way he does. If his kids can get away from him a little, they know they can get away with a lot.

Amber relies on her brothers-in-law, especially our younger brother, Rick, to help with gardening, home repairs and heavy lifting. Just like us, their kids get sick, their insurance premiums increase, their taxes are too high, and their income is too low. Will and Amber are a normal couple! Will has a professional career, benefits package, beautiful wife, brood of handsome sons, mortgage, credit cards, vegetable garden, lots of car seats, and a minivan (I'd say my little brother has been fully domesticated). He has spoken to thousands of young people about what choosing to *run the race* means and what 'the prize' really is. Will and Amber are living in the 90s – the place of freedom.

My friend, Vance Anderson, who has lived most of his life in a wheelchair says, "Life is a bit like school, except that God gives us the tests first; we get to study for them afterwards. Truly, from treasures disguised as infirmities come our greatest strengths."

My brother, Will, was aptly named. He refused to walk away from his experience empty handed. He and his family have paid a bitter price; but they did not leave their purchase on the counter. His purchase, paid for in pain, is worth every penny. By choosing not to focus on the grim circumstances, he used his *will* to alter his perspective. He now cashes in on what is ultimately worth many times the price of experience. Just like us, Will strives daily to run his race, and win the prize – freedom.

> *"He who learns must suffer. And even in our sleep, pain that cannot forget falls drop by drop upon the heart. And in our own despair, against our will, comes wisdom to us by the awful grace of God."*
> ~ *Aeschylus*

*Having someone believe in me
did not make my path easy.
It made it possible.*

Proving 'em Right

Brab's Story

"Children are likely to live up to what you believe of them."
~ Lady Bird Johnson

I stretched nervously behind the starting line, my pre-race ritual nearly complete. I politely nodded to my fellow competitors, some of the best steeplechasers in the world. Could I really do this? Could I? As I finished my final warm up stride I thought of Mom. The starter called us to the line ... I thought of my teacher, Mrs. Anderson ... I crouched poised ... "Runners set ..." I thought of Coach Artemis ... The starting pistol went off with a sharp "crack ..." I fairly threw myself into the race ... I had a lot to prove ...

I was born child number five, smack in the middle of nine children. We always figured our folks had a large family so that we kids could provide cheap child labor.

Our family operated a large dairy farm in West Layton, Utah. There were 300 Holstein cows plus 50 little Jerseys to sweeten the milk. We milked, not twice but three times a day (increases milk production by 11%). There were also what seemed a bazillion bawling, pushing, shoving calves to be hand-fed morning and night.

We cultivated 400 acres of row crop – most of it was corn for feed silage. We also grew a cash crop: fresh cucumbers and sweet corn, and beans, peas, tomatoes and onions. We hauled wheat straw, pitched manure out of stalls, and stomped silage in the pit. It was a lot of hard work, and not much fun at times, but we gained a strong work ethic and have some good memories of time spent together in the fields.

I was barely out of grade school when my dad fulfilled his lifelong dream of owning a cattle ranch. He traded his ground in Layton for an 1100 acre spread near Salmon, Idaho; a ranch called the Keystone. We picked rocks after the spring plowing, changed sprinkler pipe and hauled hay in the summer, fed cattle all winter and did a few other comparatively unpleasant chores I'd just as soon not discuss.

My father had been raised in a tough home environment. He was a better father to us than his father was to him; still, the only way he knew how to raise us was by our backsides. It was pretty rough. I don't mean to be hard on him; he is a good man with a good heart. However, his parenting methods were harsh. We were well acquainted with his black leather belt and seldom received any positive affirmation.

My personality clashed with my father's from the beginning. He often stuck his finger in my face and growled, "Brad, you are the laziest of my nine kids."

Perhaps he was trying to motivate me when he told me I had a bad attitude, was worthless and would never amount to much. He was pretty convincing though and I set out to prove him right.

When I started school, I was the shortest, skinniest, and curliest-headed kid on the playground. My classmates had a lot of fun calling me, "Shorty, Shorty" or "Curly, Curly." And what do you think they called me because I was skinny? "Skinny, Skinny?" Nope, they called me "Chicken Bones."

Adding to my already dismal self-perception was the fact that I couldn't keep up academically. While other students were sailing through their three R's – Readin' Ritin' and 'Rithmetic – I was struggling to understand just one "Я" — the letter R. I didn't understand P or B or C or K either.

A and T and V are okay because they are symmetrical and can't be turned backwards. But the others can – and as often as not, I did exactly that. My own name B-r-a-d posed serious problems. When I tried to spell it in class it came out "Brab." The kids fell over laughing. It wasn't funny to me, but I tried not to let on that it mattered much. I already knew I was dumb. One of my close friends to this day still calls me "Brab." I'd make fun of his name too, but you can't turn any of the letters backwards in "Tom."

In the second grade, my teacher (who must have understood something about the power of perception) took some time with me and discovered that little Brad Barton could not tell the difference between the number 2 and the number 5. E's and 3's, 9's and P's, d's and b's are difficult to deal with as well. These tricky symbols combined to form a serious barrier to my comprehension of math, reading, writing and spelling – skills critical for success in our modern world and vital to healthy self-perception.

As you may have guessed, I have lysdexia – uh, I mean, *dyslexia*. It didn't help my negative self perception to realize that not only was I an underweight underachiever, I now had a mental problem – a "learning disability" they called it. I called it "stupidity."

I actually did understand the concepts of these letters and numbers but couldn't relate the conception in my brain to the physical symbols on paper. So I looked, sounded and felt stupid. I never imagined amounting to much because of how I was treated by my father and my peers. I was trouble in the making. I possessed such disability, such lack of belief… well, I was the epitome of an at-risk kid.

*H*owever, one elementary teacher, Mrs. Anderson, looked beyond my annoying Attention Deficit Disorder and distracting hyperactivity and began to identify the source of my difficulty. My showing off to other kids by writing backwards set her to thinking. Extra attention was paid, special tests administered, and she proved herself right – that I wasn't the dumb kid I thought I was.

Actually, it was the other way around. Mrs. Anderson decided I was smart, then encouraged me until I began proving her right. She took time to teach me to better connect symbols with meanings, taught me tricks to distinguish the similarities, and showed me clever ways to remember my new skills. Slowly, but surely, the enigma "arithmetic" began to make sense. I also began to read and even to spell a bit.

Mrs. Anderson consistently demanded more from me, often pointed out my improvements – and I continued to prove her right. I began to suspect that "learning disability" might not mean "stupid." It seems that I could remember my mother saying things about me being smart, maybe even worth something, but her voice wasn't as loud as my dad's – or especially mine.

Dyslexia is not something a young person grows out of. As a youth, I did not possess the maturity to put this challenge in its proper perspective. Now I do. I now see it as big, fat inconvenience. I still don't spel wel, my penmanship is questionable and I am not a fast reader. I have learned to adjust to the nuisance of it all. I still take a bit of light-hearted teasing from my wife or one of my readers when I manage the occasional "Brab" while hastily autographing one of my books.

Back up. Read that last sentence again. Can you imagine what this teacher, and other teachers and coaches like her, did for me? *Signing one of my books?* In high school I could barely read; now I am a published author! I perceived myself as defective and the "facts" proved it. My teacher perceived me as talented, perhaps even gifted and she proved those facts by altering my reality. Can you imagine what would have happened to me if my self-perception had not changed?

In junior high, I attended special education classes where the alternative teaching methods and the one-on-one attention was perfect for me – but I dreaded the closing bell at the end of class. Our teasing, taunting peers had some very cruel labels for us special ed' kids. Walking out of that classroom into a sea of junior high school students was like running the gauntlet at an Iroquois convention. The three "R's became Readin', Ritin' and Ridicule.

Nevertheless, because (thanks to Mrs. Anderson) my perception of self had already begun a slight shift upward, I didn't give up. I didn't run with the wrong crowd. Then, after another long summer of changing sprinkler pipes and hauling hay, I returned to the scene. Decked out in a new pair of jeans and new backpack, I began my first year of high school, thinking maybe, just maybe, this could be a whole new world.

It wasn't. Not at first.

I stepped off the bus with cautious optimism. At 4'9" and 82 pounds – two pounds of it thick curly hair – I was not Joe College. Kids did not come running to embrace me as their new buddy. They circled me like a pack of wolves, poked at me and asked each other, "What is it?"

The ridicule of the previous year continued unabated. The best I could hope for to improve my station was to be appointed school mascot. Even today my eldest son, Jacob, loves to find old school pictures of me and laugh hysterically. When the thrill wears off, he brings his friends home to join in and the fun begins anew.

For days I walked around dejected, feeling that this was going to be even worse than Jr. High. Then my attitude shifted a bit more. I took matters into my own hands. I decided to become (drumroll) an athlete.

I announced my intention by signing up for tryouts. Instead of getting a little respect, the teasing escalated. *"Oh, no! Look out! Little Barton is going out for the team. We're really scared. Everybody run!"*

What sport do you suppose I signed up for? Well, what do you do when you are 4' 9" and 82 pounds including hair? I signed up for the wrestling team. Why not? Wrestling seemed the ideal choice. I would be competing against kids my own size. I soon found two glaring problems with my plan.

Problem #1: *There was no one my size.* The lowest weight class in Idaho was 98 pounds. Though by the start of the season I had bulked up to a threatening 83 pounds, I was still 15 pounds under the lowest weight class, which put me nearly four weight classes under weight. Wrestling even one class above weight is very difficult. *Four* classes above weight ... well ... you understand problem #1.

Problem #2: The 98 pound weight class in Idaho that year was owned by state champion Kip French. People spoke his name in hushed tones. The very mention of his name struck fear to the hearts of his competitors state-wide. Kip French was a monster, virtually undefeatable. He became my nemesis. He also became my best friend. We were teammates. Kip needed someone to practice with and I was the only one anywhere near his weight. There was no way I could beat him, or even offer him much of a workout, but I got the job anyway.

Can you imagine the carnage? Every practice he would draw blood. He would rip me apart, tear my limbs off and stack 'em like cordwood. Then he'd help me up off the blood-soaked mat, slap me on the back (torture in and of itself) and say, "Great match, buddy." "Sure," I thought, "Great for whom?" (My kids still ask to see the scars.)

Even though the first part – "great match" – was a blatant lie, I began to believe the "buddy" part. Without my realizing it, Kip French, my peer, my classmate, my hero, was also becoming my buddy. His perception of me being his comrade was slowly thawing the perma-frost of my self-perception. I was not only a friend of a "cool" guy, I was his equal. I had become an athlete!

I weighed in at 82 or 83 lbs., depending on what I had for breakfast. I was truly in a class by myself – rather I would have been except there was no such class. The state of Idaho did not recognize that there were wrestlers that small. It is sorta' like a three pound dinosaur; we know they existed, but we don't really know what to make of them. Does the name "dinosaur" – *Thunder Lizard* – really fit a tiny creature that could fit in the palm of your hand? And does the title "wrestler" or "athlete" really fit a skinny little kid called "Brab?"

With Kip owning the 98 lb. weight class, the only varsity choice for me was to wrestle at 105 lbs. Why? Because we didn't have anyone on the team that size. So, while Kip owned the 98 lb. class because he was awesome, I owned the 105 lb. class because I was a fool. I chose to compete – at serious risk of life and limb. Why did I take the risk? I was a personal friend of Kip French. I was an athlete. I could handle it.

As it turned out, I actually did manage to win two matches my freshman year – *both by forfeit*. The opposing schools didn't have an athlete at the 105 lb. weight class to compete against. As I stepped confidently onto the mat, the referee raised my right arm triumphantly toward the ceiling as the crowd went completely

– well, silent. This could have been the end of my athletic career. No real victories and no apparent chance in a sport where I simply didn't measure up.

*T*hen George Artemis, an old Greek wrestler, took the stage. Coach Artemis was born in the old country on the isle of Crete. His family immigrated to the USA when he was a small boy. I met him as he approached the end of his career as an educator. He had heavy gray eyebrows, broad muscular shoulders; a thick cauliflower ear and other battle scars from his college wrestling days. Wrestling was an Olympic event before the Romans ever came to town. The Greeks invented it, the Romans promoted it, Coach Artemis loved it.

George Artemis had been my middle school principal. I did some "hard time" in his office the previous year. I was certain about his perception of me, at least I thought so, and when I discovered that he was also the high school wrestling coach, my heart turned to lead. I imagined him thinking, "Oh no, not this impertinent kid! How am I going to get rid of him? I don't want him in my hair four more years."

By the way, I failed to mention that I compensated for my small stature with my big mouth. Nothing got past Brab, the hyperactive class clown. Way too often my big brother John risked his "cool" to rescue me, his clueless little brother, from yet another misadventure brought on by my mouthing off to the wrong guy. However, the day I attempted to give the senior middle linebacker, Richard Hurpts, a wedgie, I was on my own.

Back to Coach Artemis. I kept as far away from my tough old Greek wrestling coach as I could. I wasn't going to mess this one up. I let him do his job without any brilliant commentaries from me.

After a couple weeks of doing my best to stay out of his way, I had a fateful run-in with him. I was headed toward the lockers after a particularly uninspiring workout, when the heavy hand of doom clamped onto my shoulder and pulled me aside. "Brad ..."

I fought the urge to duck. I stood my ground. I pulled myself up to my full 4'9," ready for whatever was coming. I didn't know exactly what I had done or failed to do, but I was sure there was something. I was equally sure it was my fault.

Coach Artemis stuck his finger in my face – the same way my father used to – and said, "You ...

...You, I will make a champion!"

Me? I looked around, not believing that Coach George Artemis was saying this to me. A champion? I thought he hated me!

"Everyone is born a champion," Coach Artemis growled. "You were too, young man. Champions are born and then unmade. You have been unmade, Mr. Barton, and we are going to make you again. You and I are going to make you a champion."

I didn't believe him; but he was Coach Artemis. Something in me shifted and I decided to see if I could prove him right. In an instant, this broad-shouldered, thick-necked no-nonsense wrestling coach became my personal mentor. I didn't know it then, but his perception of me, enhanced the slow momentum started by Mrs. Anderson, and slowly my life began to turn around.

Artemis perceived that I was a champion before I could possibly see it myself. He had things to tell me about me that I had never heard before; positive things that I couldn't possibly believe …

… or could I? Having someone believe in me did not make my path easy. It made it possible. There was a lot – a lot – of hard work ahead. I had a ton of negative self-perception to overcome. I daily questioned my right to even be on the team, much less be a champion; but Coach Artemis had accurately perceived who I was. Despite my outward appearance and goof-off reputation, he established my right to be a champion and I began the long, long road to proving him right.

A few weeks later, he approached me, "Brad, your grades aren't good enough. You are going to have to work harder in school."

"But I'm not very smart, Coach."

Coach stared at me for a long moment, pretending to be enraged by my comment. His heavy white Greek eyebrows grew together like thunderclouds and lightning flashed from his dark eyes.

I wondered if the high school cheerleaders would cry at my graveside.

"Brad Barton!" Artemis said so gently you could hear it reverberate off the ceiling of the gym. "Never, never say that again! You are just as smart as you need to be!"

"But Coach, it takes me twice as long to read a book," I protested, quite sure that those would be my last words.

"Then read twice as long – that's what champions do."

"But, Coach, I have to study twice as hard to get a passing grade."

"Then study twice as hard – that's what champions do – and you are a champion, Brad Barton."

He paused for a long moment, then very softly said. "The only thing you think you are any good at, Brad, is putting yourself down. You are always trying to be funny by talking bad about yourself, and we are changing that – starting now! Champions don't talk that way about themselves – or anyone else – and you are a champion."

I began to understand that he was not going to accept my excuses. He perceived greatness in me that I did not know I possessed and demanded commensurate performance. "I need you eligible young man, and you can do it – you will do it."

He turned on his heel and walked away leaving me to wonder at the feelings that welled up inside me. I had heard only one thing: "I need you ..."

Coach needs me? He needs *me*? I did my chores that night in a daze, overjoyed that this man whom I held in such awe actually needed me. I became a champion – because Coach said I was – and he was depending on me.

I began to behave accordingly. I began proving him right. In the 1950's Earl Nightingale said that to become what we want to be we should act as if we were that already. That meant I should train as if I were a champion – and I did.

I didn't just exercise physically, I also trained my mind and spirit by reading motivational books and listening to inspirational tapes that my cousin, Dr. Richard Barton happily provided. I absorbed Zig Zigler. I digested Earl Nightingale. I drew inspiration from Dale Carnegie, Dan Clark, the small but powerful Biblical King David – and U.S. Olympic 3000 meter Steeplechase medalist, George Young. I discovered visual imagery, goal setting, and self-motivation. I had never heard these concepts before and they spoke directly to my heart.

I began to not just become, but to *be* who my coach perceived me to be. I had not won a single award or one second of acclaim from anyone, but I became a champion.

Coach was an incredible mentor. Even when he was correcting my style or technique (or attitude), I could feel his faith in me and his constant approval of my efforts. Any doubts I had about my potential had to be set aside. There was no way I could let my coach down. Not only did I begin to develop as a wrestler, I started to believe that maybe, just maybe, I could be a little better student.

Then, one day, he did it again. "Brad, you are going to college." College? How could I ever go to college?

"But, Coach, I can't go to col..." then, seeing those white thundercloud eyebrows move menacingly closer together, I quickly changed my phrasing "Coach, how could I go to college?"

"You are going to college," he repeated as matter-of-factly as one would order a pizza.

"College?" I thought, "Me? Yeah, that's pretty dang funny. Coach starts out a principal then he becomes a coach, now he's a comedian!"

I put together a carefully worded and highly intelligent response: "Huh?"

"We'll talk about it later," he said bluntly and blew the whistle for practice to start – and the conversation to end.

"Wow. I am going to college." I didn't know how, but Coach said so; therefore it was so. For the first time in my young life I felt hope. Not the kind of hope that I'd get a sled or bicycle for Christmas, or that a certain girl might like me; this wasn't "kid stuff" this was real hope. Hope for a brighter tomorrow began to burn in me. Maybe someday Brad Barton could actually be somebody. I couldn't wait to tell someone.

My dad was the first person I saw when I got home from practice. It was late; he was tired; my timing wasn't great, "Dad, Dad, you're never gonna' believe this! My wrestling coach told me that I can go to college!"

"Are you joking?" he retorted, "Look at your grades – you'll be lucky to even graduate high school." As he turned and walked away from me to do his chores, I heard him mumble, "We could never afford something like that anyway."

At practice the following week, I was glum and dejected. My new sense of hope and freedom – represented by the possibility that I could go to college – was torn from my grasp before I had even had a chance to hold it in my hand.

I didn't know what to do; so after practice I told Coach about my father's reaction. Without hesitation, and without saying that my father was wrong, he told me that I could earn an athletic scholarship.

He knew how I struggled with my grades, but told me that *athletic* scholarships were available for top-notch athletes. He told me that was exactly what I was becoming – and if I kept on improving, and worked on my grades as well, an athletic scholarship could be my ticket to college.

George Artemis wasn't given to building false hope. He had taken time to watch me and learn my strengths. He knew I had the physical talent and the heart to do what he said I could do.

Before every wrestling meet, this old Greek Orthodox Catholic led us in prayer. Every time my name was called out to begin a match, he'd grab my shoulders, square me off, look me in the eyes and say, "I love you, Brad!" Then he'd kiss me on the forehead, whip me around, slap me on the backside and yell, "now get out there and wrestle like a champ!"

I earned All-State wrestling honors three years in a row but although I worked my heart out, I never won a state wrestling championship for this man who believed in me and whom I admire so greatly (I regretted this more for him than for me) but I took the confidence, the work ethic, and that powerful positive self perception that Coach blessed my life with and made my dream – and his for me – come true.

*I*t was through running that I actually earned my ticket to college. My best friend and wrestling buddy, Kip French, talked me into trying out for cross-country as a sophomore. (I think he was getting tired of cleaning my blood off the mat.) He was a junior at the time and was also running cross-country. (He later admitted that he just wanted someone else on the team he could beat.) In my first race, he beat me by a full minute. I closed the margin between us to just two seconds in the next race. In our third race, I out-kicked him by two seconds. He never beat me again. He never even came close. He said I could run – and *I proved him right.*

Maybe Kip's contribution wasn't as obvious as that of my teachers and coaches who believed in me, but the long lasting impact of his positive belief in who I was and what I could do is immeasurably important in whatever I may ultimately achieve. This former nemesis made a huge difference in my life, even though he was just a kid like me. He was as proud of my beating him as he was of his own considerable athletic accomplishments. Of course, to this day, Kip takes all the credit for my success as a runner and the scholastic achievements it led to. I let him be right.

Coach Artemis was always proud of me. I still don't know if he ever took any credit for my success. I doubt that it matters to him. In the style of the true mentor, he handed me off to someone who would take me to the next level – cross-country coach Zane Abbott.

Coach Abbot had a totally different style. He never said "I love you, Brad" or kissed me on the forehead (I think he read the memo from the legal department) but he showed respect and appreciation for my efforts and the success I brought to the team. He worked hard to make his commitment to the team pay off and expected each of his athletes to do the same. Skipping even one of coach Abbot's creative and fun workouts was unthinkable. It was also entirely unacceptable. He found a way to make each of his runners feel that they played an important role. Like Artemis, he saw in me a champion and expected me to prove him right.

Every teacher, every coach, had their own style; but each of them added measurably to building the success of this once distracted dyslexic little kid.

My dad played an important part as well. As my athletic prowess began to emerge, he started paying more attention to me. He accompanied me to important races and spoke of my accomplishments with pride. When I was a senior in high school, he began correspondence with Chick Hislop, head coach of Weber State University's track and cross-country teams, one of the top ranked programs in the nation. My dad persuaded him to fly to Idaho to watch me compete. Although Coach Hislop still denies it, I know for a fact that he took advantage of my dad's free transportation offer so that he could look at another Idaho runner he'd been following.

That weekend I owned the Idaho State Cross-Country Championship – setting the course record and beating that other runner by 50 seconds – and Hislop recruited me instead. If not for my father, I would never even have been on Hislop's radar.

Gruff, no-nonsense Coach Chick Hislop built on the foundation of self-esteem and confidence that my former mentors had planted within me. With his encouragement – usually communicated in the delicate style of an angry Marine Corps drill sergeant – I excelled.

Chick Hislop believed in me not only as an athlete but as a person, a student and eventually a friend. He not only insisted that

I could be a great athlete, he convinced me that I could be a great student as well if I would just do what Coach Artemis had told me earlier; read twice as long and study twice as hard.

So I did. It wasn't easy, but not only did I earn the Weber State University Athlete of the Year Award, I also graduated with gold tassels – Cum Laude!

This was pretty amazing to this undersized, dyslexic, late-blooming, underachiever; but it was not at all surprising to my mother, my coaches and teachers, and peer mentors like Kip French. Knowingly or unknowingly they had applied the magic power of positive perception and watched while I proved them right.

In a book called *Earning an A with Kids* that I co-authored with Coach Rick Larsen and his high school daughter, Kylee, we reveal that this kind of effective mentoring can be conscientiously developed by applying what we call the Ten A's. It is, in effect, the magic formula behind the power of positive perception. It is like alchemy. It turns lead into gold. It helps move kids past their illusions of inadequacy and limiting beliefs. The ten A's are acceptance, acknowledgement, acclamation, action, approval, appreciation, appraisal, achievement, accessibility, and allegiance.

Parents, your kids may have greater potential than you could ever imagine. Who they are and who they ultimately become is never more powerfully affected than by the way you perceive them.

Teachers and coaches, do you realize your classrooms are filled with greatness? You can make a lot of mistakes with kids but if you see them as wonderful – not just potentially, but right now – they will likely become as you perceive them, even if their current behavior or attitudes about themselves don't quite match up. Just let them know how you perceive them, and wait for them to prove you right.

It is easy to believe in achievers and mentor the obviously bright sons and daughters, successful students and athletes. It is easy to see their greatness and they usually accept your praise and affirmation. Sometimes they even expect it. But there is also greatness buried in the resource student, the also-ran, and the rebellious underachiever.

Every child, even that disruptive class clown on the back row, can make a significant contribution. Tell them – no, show them – who they are and watch for opportunities to praise them for proving you right. They may remember you for the rest of their lives, as I remember my teachers and coaches – or they may not; but whether they remember or ever acknowledge you, or even know what you did, *you* will know. Through your magic power of positive perception you will shift and change their reality – and their lives – and the lives of those they touch – just like my mentors did for me.

*O*n a warm spring evening in 1991, as the Weber State University athletic banquet reached its grand finale, Athletic Director, Dick Hennen, stood to announce the Male Athlete of the Year. As he revealed that I was the recipient of this prestigious award, he turned the microphone over to my coach. Chick Hislop told the assembled student athletes and alumni that the recipient of this award was about to earn All-American honors at the upcoming NCAA Track and Field National Championships. No pressure here!

Seven days later at The University of Oregon's famous Hayward Field, I stretched nervously behind the starting line, my pre-race ritual nearly complete. I politely nodded to my fellow competitors, some of the best steeplechasers in the world. Hislop had already promised the crowd that I would be an All-American at the conclusion of this race. Could I really do this? Could I? As I finished my final warm up stride, I thought of Mom. The starter called us to the line … I thought of my teacher, Mrs. Anderson … I crouched poised … "Runners set …" I thought of Coach Artemis … The starters pistol went off with a sharp "crack" and I fairly threw myself into the race. I had a lot to prove – I had to prove 'em right.

> *"What we have done for ourselves alone dies with us. What we have done for others and the world remains and is immortal."* ~ Albert Pine

*Under the circumstances,
my chances looked bleak.
But Hislop had trained me
to look beyond the
illusion of mere
circumstances and onto a
place of conviction and power.*

Hislopology

Keeping Responsibility *on Track*

"We have the Bill of Rights. What we need is a Bill of Responsibilities." ~ *Bill Maher*

*T*he pace was too hot. My legs and arms were turning to mush. My throat and lungs burned with a dry flame. A hard frown decorated Coach Hislop's lined face as his runners passed the six-mile mark and he casually checked his stopwatch. I searched desperately for eye contact that never came. There would be no reprieve; not yet.

It was late September, 1987. I was back at Weber State University in the foothills of the beautiful Wasatch mountain range in Northern Utah. I had just completed a two-year religious commitment as a Mormon missionary in Northern California. I was anxious to prove that I deserved the athletic scholarship Coach Chick Hislop had held over for me. Spreading the good news of Christ meant long, dedicated hours of consecrated service. For those two years I had walked a million miles, but not run a single step. I was paying for it now.

With too much pride to back down, I soldiered on through mounting fatigue. Having no base of fitness to draw from, I had no staying power. If I did have a future running career at Weber State, it was going to take some time to develop.

I wondered if Hislop had forgotten about me completely. The thought spawned new anguish to my already sensory-overloaded mind.

I heard the van pulling up behind us as my fit teammates mocked me good-naturedly, "Coach is trying to kill off another new guy!"

Finally, the gruff but blessed words, "Barton, get in the van." I tried to look indifferent as I coasted to a stop on shaky legs and casually (but oh so gratefully) climbed into the front passenger seat. My studied "cool" disappeared as the dry coughing from abused lungs immediately began.

Two years had passed since Hislop and I had spent any time together. I wanted badly to converse, to connect, to give my coach a different impression of me than I had in the year I'd spent struggling as an underweight, physically immature freshman.

After a few minutes of catching me up on Weber State's recent accomplishments, and speaking of the fall recruiting efforts, Coach fell silent. I tried to keep the conversation moving. "How 'bout them Jazz?" I quipped, referring to our state's professional basketball franchise. The Utah Jazz team was finally getting good. They were beginning a ten-year run that would eventually culminate in two trips to the NBA finals. Their early success had created no small anticipation at the start of that 1987-88 season.

I questioned Coach Hislop about various aspects of the team, the stars, the coaching staff and his view of their chances for the present season. Hislop's answers were polite but brief. I then mentioned how much fun it was listening to the Jazz famous play-by-play announcer "Hot" Rod Hundley, whose quick wit and gift for analogy were legendary. Coach remained silent as I rambled on about a particular call and the funny way Hot Rod had handled the announcing.

Hislop's silence continued. I asked him what he thought of this broadcaster who had so caught my imagination. Hislop sat thinking for a long moment before responding, "I think Hot Rod Hundley is the worst thing that has ever happened to Utah athletics," he said matter-of-factly.

Taken aback and feeling a little embarrassed about my enthusiasm, but also a little defensive of this great commentator I so enjoyed, I pressed for an explanation. I got one – and yet another dose of Hislopology.

In Hislop's opinion, Hundley's play-by-play reporting included far too many references to faulty and inaccurate officiating. His frequent bemoaning of the officials' poor calls took the focus off the talent and skill of the players, off the competition, off the exhilaration of the contest, and onto the necessary but ancillary officiating. Hislop felt that Hundley at times took this to such an extreme that the games outcome appeared to be influenced more by the call than by the playing of the game.

As the Utah Jazz fan base became accustomed to the focus on the call, this complaining attitude filtered out to include college, prep, and even little league programs in a variety of sports. Hislop was deeply concerned about this growing tendency away from personal accountability and onto a mentality of fatalism and avoidance of responsibility.

Coach cared very deeply about the game – the entire game, not just the calls. Games include many calls but the calls are not the game. "Basketball is like life;" Hislop explained, "It is a series of interrelated events or 'plays.' We move the ball forward from one play to the next in a never-ending march toward the final buzzer. Along the way, opinions, judgments, and decisions that effect us significantly are made by people other than us – decisions that we have little or no control over. Conclusions are drawn, judgments are made, verdicts are reached and sentences passed that seem to alter the course of our lives."

Hislop continued, "It is all too easy to become focused on the call and thereby lose sight of the game. Rather than wasting time and energy concentrating on the call – something over which we have little control – we should be anxiously engaged in the playing of the game."

Hislop's gripe was that this particular commentator's popularity and influence created a collective consciousness of the call and got Utah sports fans attention off the scoring process. A call is a call. You might consider it a bad call or a good call but it is neither; it is just a call and it is part of the game. Better a bad call than no call at all; the game cannot move forward without it.

As I sat next to him in the van, absorbing my coach's incredible insight, a familiar feeling returned once again with sickening clarity. My mind flashed back to late February 1984, the Boise

State University Athletic Pavilion, my senior year in high school, and that *dirty, rotten, no-good referee.*

*I*t was the semifinal round of the Idaho State Wrestling Championships. I had been wrestling flawlessly and was now only two matches away from achieving my long-time dream of winning a state title. Late in the third and final period of the match, I was losing to a tough opponent 4 to 3; but he was in trouble. My fitness level was better than his and I knew I could prevail. Going into that final period with a one point lead, my opponent fell into a difficult to deal with illicit stalling posture. Throughout the period, I tried desperately to force his hand. I even placed myself in jeopardy to get him to do something, anything but defensively retreat and literally hold on for the win. The referee continued to turn a blind eye to my opponent's illegal delaying tactics.

With just seconds remaining, I successfully initiated a complicated roll-out maneuver called a "reverse." This change of possession should have earned me two points and the victory. However, the referee called the move out-of-bounds and reset my badly stalling opponent in the advantage position; no points, no lead, and no time left on the clock for another assault. He blew the whistle for the match to continue just moments before the clock ran out on my chance at a state championship, a finals match against an athlete I'd beaten earlier in the season. The match was over.

I wearily removed the colored band from my ankle as my opponent stood exhausted – his arm held high in victory by the black and white striped official while his teammates cheered. I felt sick. This match should have been mine. But for a poor call by an inattentive referee, it would have been mine.

My father was incensed! He came out of the stands with his huge state-of-the-art JVC camcorder with instant playback on the tiny built-in back and white pop-out monitor. He pleaded with the referee to take a look. Probably curious to get a look at such amazing new technology, the referee walked over and watched the replay of the final seconds of my match. Dad showed him the footage with vocal commentary three times before the contrite referee turned to my father and frankly said, "It looks like I made a mistake. I'm very sorry."

He then turned back to the mat and called two grapplers forward for the coin toss to start the next match.

We stood stunned. That was it? My coach, George Artemis, walked over with tears in his eyes and told me he loved me. He then set to work preparing me for a difficult afternoon.

It is true that this poor call cost me a shot at the championship. It was a bitter blow. I was placed in the consolation bracket. This meant two tough matches within a couple of hours just for a chance at third place. Instead of meeting these opponents on fair and equal ground, I chose to carry the ghost of my unjust semi-final match into the consolation contests. As a result, I faced two foes at a time, my opponent and my own anger and self-pity.

Sometimes we do carry a heavier burden because of someone else's mistake. That is a hard reality. However, carrying the additional burden of anger and self pity adds needlessly to the heavy load we already bear. How much better it would have been for me to let the call remain the call and get on with the game.

I did win those last two matches, ending my career with a respectable third place finish. However, the bronze medal I received that evening in ceremony was due more to great coaching than on my willingness to face my reality, forget the call and keep myself focused on the game. I would have been well served to remember the special meditation that is an important part of twelve-step substance abuse recovery programs. It is credited to theologian Reinhold Niebuhr and is known as the Serenity Prayer.

> "God grant me the serenity
> to accept the things I cannot change
> the courage to change the things I can
> and the wisdom to know the difference."

I still enjoy listening to the lightning fast, clever, smooth drone of "Hot" Rod Hundley. He is still my favorite. However, when Hot Rod sets in on the poor officiating, I smile to myself and remember the life lesson Coach Hislop taught me so many years ago.

Shortly after publication of the first edition of this book, I received a phone call from Coach Hislop. I'd sent him a copy as my gift just days after the announcement of his retirement from Weber State University. He phoned to congratulate me on my accomplishment and had some very nice things to say about this book. He also requested a face-to-face meeting. I felt a familiar foreboding, but reminded myself that I was no longer running laps under his critical eye.

Two days later, we sat together in my office and caught up on old times. We spoke of the direction Weber's track program was headed and how excited he was about the new coaching staff.

After an hour or so of talking track, he leaned over to an open box of brand new *Beyond Illusions*. He picked up two books, tossed one to me and said, "turn to page 110." I thought to myself, *here it comes*. After finding the page and reading aloud the suspect line, he leaned back in his chair, looked up at the vaulted ceiling in my office and with a grin he said, "I'm gonna – how shall I say this – 'Hislopology' you again, Brad." He then proceeded to impart yet another of his many life lessons.

The offending line read: *"It is true that this poor call cost me a shot at the championship."* Hislop suggested that I re-think that line. He reminded me that there are many questionable calls and stressed that when one comes at the end of a match or game it appears that this one call is entirely responsible for the game's outcome. "Brad," he grinned wryly, *"this is another one of your illusions."*

He paused for effect, leaned forward, and bluntly asked why I hadn't attempted the roll-out move in question much earlier in the final period of the match. "That ref' didn't cost you a shot at the title – *you* did."

He said it sounded like I'd spent the period more concerned about what was going on in the mind of the referee than on what was going on in my own mind. He suggested I should have stopped trying to officiate the match and got busy wrestling it instead. "When you can look in the mirror and honestly say that you made fewer mistakes in that match than the official did, *then* you can complain about the call." Hislop paused again for effect, "Until then, it's just a call."

Hislopology is rooted and grounded in this legendary coach's conviction that we must keep our eyes always on the game. Calls are interesting, curious little scorecards but not particularly relevant to the successful playing of the game. The way we play the game is the only thing we have control over – it is the only thing that matters.

Have you ever written yourself a To Do list? Armed with a thoughtfully prepared To Do list, you find yourself more focused on your game and less distracted by lousy calls. A To Do list concentrates your attention and, consequently, your efforts. It is no secret that this is an effective tool for increasing productivity. Good focus, great game! (Some people are so obsessive about their To Do lists that when they accomplish a task that isn't on their list, they add it just so they can enjoy the satisfaction of checking it off.)

How about an idea not so well known? This idea can also have a dramatic effect on how well we play the game. Business author, Joe Calloway, suggests that along with our To Do list, we should create a To *Stop Doing* list. What a novel idea – novel and effective.

At the top of this list of things to *stop* doing is to stop putting too much attention and energy on lousy calls. As long as we focus on the poor call we are diverted from our game. Don't get me wrong, wrongful accusations; accidents; misjudgments; poor decisions by others that affect us do cost us. Sometimes they cost us dearly. But, in life, they never cost us the game – as long as we stay focused on the game and our attention and energy are not misdirected by the call. Calloway invites us to let that stuff go – just let it go. We'll play better without the dead weight.

Misdirection is one of the most valuable skills of the clever magician. My editor was taught an important lesson by someone doing jail time for drug dealing. He was only nineteen years old and already paying a heavy price for being misled by the misdirection of advertising. The young convict said that the pretty girl leaning against the brand new car is not what is important in life; but it is treated by the media as so important that some will give up their freedom by doing anything, legal or not, to get the money to have the car to get the girl – and it is all illusion.

He said, "Misdirection is accomplished by treating something important as though it isn't important and treating something that is not important as though it is."

As a magician, I use misdirection to attract my audience's attention away from the most important part of the trick. I get them to look, instead, at something less important. By clever misdirection, I am able to fool observers into believing my deception. As the young convict wisely pointed out, this notion of misdirection has application to every day living.

Have you ever given up a dream in exchange for a small desire, then walked away feeling ripped off? When we take our eyes off the prize and exchange what we want most for what we want right now, that's giving in to misdirection. In this regard, Steven Covey says, "The main thing is to keep the main thing the main thing." The thing we can do something about is the main thing.

The central doctrine of Hislopology is accepting personal responsibility. He set a high standard for us as student athletes then held us and himself to that standard. By Hislop's wristwatch, "on time" is five minutes early. He held us responsible for not just being on Hislop Time, but also being ready to contribute when we arrived. Pulling our weight and doing our part was as much a part of Weber State's track program as pulling on our track shoes and heading out of the locker room.

We ran in all types of weather. Workout schedules didn't change because of foul weather conditions; and I can remember foul weather aplenty. On a bitterly cold January afternoon, my teammates and I were milling about the locker room waiting for Coach to come up from the indoor track where he'd been working out the sprinters. The sun was out. The temperature had risen to a balmy *minus* 21 degrees Fahrenheit. It was a recovery day for us which meant an easy 10 mile run at 6:30 mile pace, followed by an indoor hurtle ritual for the steeplechase crew, then 30 minutes in the weight room. Surely, he wouldn't expect us to run outdoors on a record-breaking cold day – I mean, how could that help us recover from anything? When he arrived and saw that we hadn't left on our run as scheduled, he reprimanded us for worrying about the weather.

"But it's *really* cold out today coach," we whined.

"Then put on a few extra layers and go for a little run, that'll warm you up." he countered. Dejected, we bundled up and headed out. As we left the locker room, he said, "Boy, you all sure flunked the intelligence test today."

Hislop's coaching style combines no nonsense, focused determination and stern discipline. It is a "save your whining for your mother" environment. Complaints and excuses are not only wasted on Hislop, they can actually earn you a stern rebuke, or worse. It's better just to keep your head down and run. Run hard, without complaint.

Interval workouts at the hand of Chick Hislop are not for sissies. They are tough, most often really tough. Many times over the years, my teammates and I approached these trauma sessions sick or injured. Hislop always expected his runners to take terminal illness or arterial bleeding 'in stride' — literally. I do not remember Hislop ever telling me to go back home and get in bed where I felt I belonged. Instead, he would expect me to take my place alongside my comrades and give him whatever strength I had.

An important aspect of Hislopology is his deep belief in the adage, "What does not kill us makes us stronger." We wondered at times if we would live through some of those workouts; the toughest of which we called 'come-to-Jesus' encounters.

This was not intended as sacrilege. These were momentous events the likes of which we will tell our grandchildren. They were painful, nearly sacred experiences that brought us to a different place. My teammates and I became stronger as a result, both physically and mentally, and I believe, spiritually. We grew to accept more responsibility and to perform no matter the circumstance.

Interval workouts are tricky to figure. With fresh legs, it would seem that the first in a set would be the least difficult. This is not the case. The pace is so darn fast that it takes the first interval just to get the body acclimatized to the shock of it. Interval number two is usually the easiest. By number four, things begin to get serious.

*I*t happened as we rounded the turn into the backstretch. It was interval number four, in a series of six. As we gulped in the spring air, an unfortunate bumblebee shot into my mouth and blasted straight down my throat and into my left lung. My oxygen starved body guzzled air as the sweet taste of pollen flavored the coughing fit that immediately and entirely overcame me. On hands and knees by the side of the track, I worked the startled bee from my seared lung. A raw burning sensation filled my airways as the tears began to flow. This whole scenario had carried on only a few horrible seconds when from across the track I heard the familiar roar, "Gaaaaadangit Barton, what are you doing!?"

Instinctively I knew explanation was no use. It would only make my position worse with my coach. I was an upper classman and well versed in the discipline of Hislopology. Although not my fault, this was my circumstance, and I was expected not to get caught under the weight of it. Still coughing, I took to my feet. Pollen now mixed with blood tasted heavy on my tongue.

The injustice of the assault by the bee, while I was struggling at the extreme limits of my physical capacity, produced an emotional response that surprised me and was difficult to manage. Tears flowing, I jumped back on the track, picked up speed and belatedly finished the interval. There was barely time to coast to a stop, walk back to the others, and take my place in line for the start of the next interval. Before Hislop waved us on, he shot me a knowing glance. The look was a mixture of pride, satisfaction and respect. I had passed the Hislopology test that day.

For us privileged few who have toiled under the stern gaze of a master coach, the treasure is not so much in the winning, but in the pursuit. Charles "Chick" Hislop, a man well known and deeply respected nation-wide in the track and field community, understands his role well. Though fiercely competitive, he endorses a higher ideal. He has come to know that to be unfettered by poor habit, weak constitution, and lack of responsibility, is to know true freedom. Getting beyond illusions of circumstances, bad luck, and disadvantage – that is freedom. To me, the gradual increase in one's personal freedom is ultimately what Hislopology is about.

The date was July 9th, 1992. It was the day before fellow WSU steeplechase star, Kurt Black, Coach Hislop, and I were to leave for New Orleans, host city for the USA Track and Field Olympic Trials. The hot sun bore down on my already overheated body as I stood dizzy at the line. My legs trembled in exhaustion as I sucked in the hot dry Utah summer air. Hislop stood unmoved.

"I want the first 200 meters at race pace and then you kick this in the butt and see how fast you can finish the last 400 meters. This is it now, Brad. We are simulating the gun lap of the finals. Only three make the Olympic team. Let's get it done." He nodded for me to stand on the line and firmly said, "Go!"

I went, at first under control but then at 200 meters I tossed everything I had at the final lap over hurtles. With just under 150 meters remaining, I leapt at the water barrier at full speed.

I'd negotiated this obstacle many hundreds of times over the last 8 years. This time, in extreme fatigue, I misjudged it badly. Instead of landing firmly on top of the 4 X 4 wooden beam and pushing off with momentum onto the covered water pit, my track-spiked toe barely made contact with the barrier then slipped off hard in front of it. The impact tore a deep chunk of flesh from the front of my shin bone. The velocity-charged impact shot me over the barrier and headlong into the covered water pit. I landed first on my wrist and then hard to my exposed left shoulder. When the dust settled, I lay in a heap of sweat and blood and tears.

The hospital exam revealed a fractured wrist, separated shoulder and a badly bruised, lacerated right shin. I refused the cast, preferring a lightweight, removable nylon brace. We were scheduled to leave for the Olympic Trials in the morning. Under the circumstances, my chances looked bleak. But Hislop had trained me not to operate "under" the circumstances. Winners look beyond the illusion of mere circumstance and onto a place of conviction and power. I do remember feeling great physical pain. In fact it hurt like heck. I do not remember ever considering that this could be anything but an inconvenience on the way to achieving my goal.

I competed in New Orleans that next week. In fact I ran one of the fastest 3000 meter steeplechase races of my life. Although I was not successful in making the 1992 USA Track and Field Barcelona Games team, I ultimately found myself successful in far grander pursuits. This incredible coach has given so much of his life to not only the noble sport of track and field, but also to the building of the stature, confidence and maturity of hundreds of young student athletes over the course of a brilliant 38-year career. Because of Chick Hislop and so many other enlightened mentors who blessed my life, I have been empowered to stand and face my illusions with confidence and persistence, even when events seem to conspire against me and it feels like I sucked in a bee.

"The best years of your life are the ones in which you decide your problems are your own. You do not blame them on your mother, the ecology, or the president. You realize that you control your own destiny." ~ Albert Ellis

Epilogue

So, what have you discovered *beyond illusions?*

You have seen a new way of looking at how you look at things – and discovered that your reality is often not real.

A knight in rusty armor has demonstrated the causative power of having delusions of others' grandeur. You have experienced the power of a messy five-year-old's hug and how to see with vision through the adventure of the *Poisonberry Perspective*. Earl Nightingale and Viktor Frankl and Grandma Sessions revealed to you that nothing is bad because bad is not a *thing* – it is only a *perception.*

Never again need you be the helpless hopeless victim of circumstance because you've realized that living in the 90s wins for you the best and greatest prize of all – freedom. You have discovered the magical power you have always possessed to change yourself and those around you through the art of guided perception. Your powerful new mental vocabulary will now change the world by empowering people in it.

Now it's time to follow Don Quixote into his world – a world not of delusion but a world *beyond illusion* where the power to shift perspective and perception, and thereby alter reality, transforms you and those around you positively and permanently.

You do have *the magic power of positive perception,* or as I say to my audiences, "You've got magic."

Bibliography

Allen, James. *As A Man Thinketh*. Hallmark Cards. Kansas City, 1968

Baum, Frank L. *The Wonderful Wizard of Oz*. North-South Books.
New York, 1900

Cervantes Saavedra, Miguel de. *Don Quixote de la Mancha*. (Translated by John
Rutherford) Penguin Group. New York, 2003

Covey, Stephen R. *Seven Habits of Highly Effective People*. Simon & Schuster.
New York, 1989

Davis, Ronald D. *The Gift of Dislexia*. Perigee. New York, 1994

Dyer, Wayne. *Your Erroneous Zones*. Avon Books. New York, 1977

Frankl, Viktor E. *Man's Search For Meaning*. Washington Square Press.
New York, 1985

Kranz, Gene. *Failure is not an Option*. Simon & Schuster. New York, 2000

Lewis, C.S. *The Screwtape Letters*. Bantam Books. New York, 1982

Maltz, Maxwell. *Psycho-Cybernetics*. Bantam Books. New York, 1972

Mandino, Og. *The Greatest Salesman In The World*. Fredrick Fell.
New York, 1968

Nightingale, Earl. *The Strangest Secret.* Nightingale-Conant. Niles, IL, 1957

Peck, Scott M. *The Road Less Traveled.* Simon & Schuster. New York, 1978

Shakespeare, William. *Hamlet Act II, scene ii*

Swindoll, Charles R. *Strengthening Your Grip.* Word, Inc. Dallas, 1982

The Holy Bible (King James Version)

About the Author

Who is this witty magical speaker who has audiences across the country laughin' and thinkin'? Brad Barton was a misdirected kid headed for disaster. Then he ran headlong into an old Greek wrestling coach who looked at this skinny little rebel and created an All-American athlete. He richocheted off an English teacher who took the time to read his dyslexic ramblings and created an author. He then bounced like a positive pinball from mentor to mentor all the way up to a successful happy life; a life that was designed for failure but destined for greatness ...

Whose greatness? The greatness of the kids he coaches, the teachers he teaches and the business leaders he inspires.

Brad's wife of 17 years (also his college track teammate) and their five kids (all faster'n greased lightening – it's in their DNA) enjoy being included in his message. He illustrates his points with stories from the ordinary adventures of his extraordinary family; the "Poisonberry Perspective," "That's Snot a Bad Deal," "Caught 'cha doin' it Right."

College Cum Laude graduate; All-American athlete; Member of the National Speakers Association, Brad insists that bad beginnings don't predict bad endings and disasters aren't disasters. Invite him to speak. The tricks and tales of this high-energy keynote speaker with the magical message will have you believing *you've got magic* before you can say "Shazaam!"

Brad Barton Presentations Inc.
2447 Woodland Dr.
Ogden, UT 84403
1-801-392-4088
BradBartonSpeaks.com

Brad@BradBartonSpeaks.com

About the Editor

Why would we write "about the editor?" Because he deserves it. Tom Cantrell is known for his ability to hear what authors want to say and help them say it the way they really mean to say it. That is the definition of "creative editor."

He is a presenter of ideas that challenge the standard of common thought and he gives his ideas away as fast as they come to him. Author and speaker in his own right, his greatest calling, however, is to empower others to change the world by saying the right thing at the right time to the right people in the right way.